DYNAMIC STUDIES
IN EPHESIANS

BRINGING GOD'S WORD TO LIFE

FRED A. SCHEEREN

WESTBOW
PRESS®
A DIVISION OF THOMAS NELSON
& ZONDERVAN

Scripture taken from King James Version of the Bible.

Scripture quotations marked NLT are taken from the Holy Bible, New Living Translation, copyright 1996, 2004, 2007. Used by permission of Tyndale House Publishers, Inc. Carol Stream, Illinois 60188. All rights reserved.

WestBow Press books may be ordered through booksellers or by contacting:

WestBow Press
A Division of Thomas Nelson & Zondervan
1663 Liberty Drive
Bloomington, IN 47403
www.westbowpress.com
1 (866) 928-1240

ISBN: 978-1-5127-8559-3 (sc)
ISBN: 978-1-5127-8560-9 (e)

Library of Congress Control Number: 2017906978

Print information available on the last page.

WestBow Press rev. date: 07/06/2017

DEDICATION

I DEDICATE THIS book to my lovely wife, Sally, who is a Jewish believer. She has stood by me over the years and raised our sons in our God-loving home. The comfort of sharing our friendship and our love for Christ has encouraged me greatly in creating this series of dynamic studies of various books of the Bible. Sally's participation in our small group studies has added a much deeper dimension of richness to the discussions. Thank you for sharing your heritage, training, and knowledge.

CONTENTS

I have also enjoyed the input and encouragement of my friend, Ron Jones, as I have continued to prepare these studies. Ron is a former high school principal and administrator. He is also a committed believer and daily student of God's Word. His background in education coupled with his love of God and His Word has made him a powerful force for good.

I would also like to express thanks to my good friend, Gordon Haresign, for his continued support and encouragement in my efforts to produce the Dynamic Bible Studies series. Gordon's journey began with his birth in the Belgian Congo. In the following years he was a senior executive with an international accounting firm, served in the military, labored as a Bible college professor, was instrumental in the leadership of a worldwide Bible correspondence school, and currently serves on the board of directors of Scripture Union, an international Bible-based ministry. Gordon's work as a teacher, speaker, and missionary has taken him to over 50 countries on five continents. His two most recent books, *Authentic Christianity* and *Pray for the Fire to Fall* should be required reading for all believers. Speaking of the Dynamic Bible Studies series, he has written "These are among the finest, if not the finest, inductive Bible studies available today. I strongly endorse them."

I would also like to express my appreciation to my two proof-readers. This includes:

- Cynthia Nicastro, an intelligent, ardent and devoted student of the Scriptures and a meticulous grammarian.

- My wife Sally, a Jewish believer and Ivy League educated lawyer who was law review in law school, worked for the Superior Court of the State of Pennsylvania, and is now in private practice.

May God bless you, inspire you, teach you, and change your life for the better as you work through these lessons.

Welcome to what I hope you find to be a most enjoyable and enlightening study of a letter written by one of the most intelligent and educated men in history. This man's life was changed from that of a religious zealot to one of the most dedicated followers of the Jewish Messiah. This letter is part of the group of documents that today is known as "The Bible" and is referred to as the Book of Ephesians.

As we consider how this book of the Bible fits into the whole of the New Testament and the Tanakh (the name used by Jews for the Old Testament, used here to emphasize the Jewishness of the Scriptures), we need to realize a number of things. We should stand in awe of this collection of 66 books, written over thousands of years by at least 40 different authors. Every detail of the text is there by design. It explains history before it happens, and comes to us from outside the dimension of time. It is, in short, the most amazing, most authenticated, and most accurate book available in the world.

If this claim is not strong enough, add to it the indisputable fact that the words contained therein have changed more lives than any others now in existence.

While the Judeo-Christian Scriptures are demonstrably perfect, my prepared studies are not. There is no way I or anyone else could possibly incorporate the depth of the text into individual sessions. I simply desire to provide a vehicle for others to use in their investigation of the Scriptures as they incorporate these timeless truths into their lives.

Speaking of small groups, Dr. Chuck Missler, a former Fortune 500 CEO, said "I experienced more growth in my personal life as a believer by participating in small group bible studies than anything else." I believe you may find this to be true in your experience and encourage you to be an active participant in such a mutually supportive, biblically-based group.

GROUND RULES

I DESIGNED THE first portion of each study to encourage readers to think about their personal situation. I designed the second portion to help people understand what the text says and how it relates to the whole of Scripture. And finally, each lesson ends with a discussion designed to help people apply that lesson.

You will notice that, in most instances, I have included the citation, but not the actual text of the Scripture we are considering. I did this on purpose. I believe we all learn more effectively if we have to dig out the text itself. As a byproduct of that exercise, we become more familiar with this marvelous book.

Scripture references are preceded or followed by a question or series of questions. Again, this is on purpose. I have also found that people seem to learn most effectively when employing the Socratic Method. That is, instead of telling someone what the text says and how it relates to other texts and life, they will remember it better if they answer questions about it and ferret out the information for themselves.

In a few instances, I have inserted additional commentary or partial answers to some of the questions to help the group get the most out of the study.

It is my intention and suggestion that the various scripture references be read out loud as part of each session. Shorter passages might be read by one participant, while anything over two or three verses might serve everyone better if one member reads one verse and another reads the next until the passage is completed. This keeps everyone involved. After reading these passages, I intend that how they relate to the primary Scripture at hand in Ephesians be seriously considered. At times, this relationship seems to be available and obvious on the surface. In many other instances, the interconnectedness of the whole of Scripture and its principles are most effectively understood through deeper thought, discussion, and prayer.

In commenting on and discussing the various passages, questions, concepts, and principles in this material, it is not required that any particular person give his or her input. The reader of any passage may, but is not pressured to, give his or her thoughts to the group. This is a group participation exercise for the mutual benefit of all involved and many people in the group giving their insight into a certain verse or question will often enhance the learning experience.

I also have two practical suggestions if you work through this book in a small group setting. Every time you meet, I suggest you review the calendar and agree upon the next scheduled meeting as well as who will bring refreshments. This will help the group to run a lot more smoothly while enhancing everyone's enjoyment and expectations.

INTRODUCTION TO EPHESIANS

Today we begin what I hope you will find a most interesting and life-impacting study on the book of Ephesians. The original manuscript of this book appears to have been penned by none other than the famous Saul of Tarsus, otherwise known as the apostle Paul, between 60 and 62 A.D. At that time, this man, considered by many to have been the most intelligent and well educated individual of his day, was under house arrest in Rome.

Why, one might ask, was this important, famous, and intelligent man writing to the people in what we today regard as an insignificant town of admittedly impressive ruins in modern-day Turkey?

To gain an understanding of this we must simply take a look at the situation, place and power of this city approximately 2000 years ago. At that time Ephesus was so populous and sophisticated that it was known as "The Queen of Asia."

It was the place where the first gold and silver coins were created to facilitate commerce and was the home of the legendary Lydian King Croesus. The saying "rich as Croesus" emanates from the great wealth of the King and the city itself and was in use by the 6th century B.C.

Subsequent to the rule of Croesus the city was conquered by Alexander the Great and thereafter by the Romans.

When under Roman control, as it was at the time the letter to the Ephesians was written, the city had reached the pinnacle of its prominence. They had such a highly developed administrative structure and economic importance with their great harbor that the Romans made Ephesus the Roman capital of Asia.

In addition to its prominence in government and trade, Ephesus was well-known as a religious center. The huge Temple of Diana (Artemis), one of the "seven wonders" of the ancient world, was located there. This temple served as what some call the first bank in the world as well as a place of ritual temple prostitution. Indeed, many local artisans made a good living creating gold and silver idols of the goddess as well as of the temple itself.

So there we have it. Ephesus was the most cosmopolitan and at the same time hedonistic and pagan centers in the region during the first century A.D.

With this understanding we should also be aware that Paul had a history with this city and its citizens. He spent two years of his life there working, debating with the intellectuals, and sharing the Good News of the full life available through Jesus Christ.

His efforts led to a number of the residents experiencing a new life and subsequently changing their behavior. Instead of frequenting the temple prostitutes and buying gold idols from the city's artisans they spent more time with their families, in home Bible study groups, helping the poor, and feeding the hungry.

This change in behavior then further resulted in a severe decline in revenue to the temple, the temple harlots, and the temple priests. It was also a great blow to the large portion of the concomitant economy devoted to manufacturing and selling artifacts and idols.

This led to a great uproar against Paul and his turbulent departure from the city in 58 A.D. (See Acts 19)

However, things involving Paul and New Testament believers in Ephesus did not stop there. Those who had trusted Jesus continued in their faith and more people were added to their number. At the same time these followers of the Jewish Messiah were under great societal pressure. It is for this reason that some of the greatest writings of encouragement and instruction for believers under fire that are in use to this day come from the letter Paul wrote to the Ephesians after his departure when he was under arrest in Rome.

Many believers in Ephesus stood up to persecution and endured to victory. This continuing battle in what was a pagan stronghold was still continuing when the book of Revelation was written by the apostle John about 33 years later. This book contained a letter dictated by Jesus Christ Himself to the believers in Ephesus. (See Revelation 2:1-7)

Sadly, while many believers in Ephesus persevered to victory, many did not as alluded to in Revelation 2:5.

We now have the opportunity to learn and benefit not only from the experience of all these people, but in particular from the book of Ephesians which was instrumental in the lives of those believers who chose to forge ahead to victory. Let us also make that same choice.

Week 1

Special Privileges
Ephesians 1:1-14

Open in Prayer

Group Warm-Up Questions

How often do you compliment others?

How do you normally respond when someone compliments you?

Read: Ephesians 1:1-14

Reread: Ephesians 1:1

To whom was this letter addressed?

How was Paul made an apostle?

Chuck Smith said "no calling is better than another IF by the will of God." What do you think of his statement?

If Chuck Smith's statement is correct, are the following declarations equivalent in terms of their value? Please explain.

"Tom, a corporate executive, by the will of God."

"Sally, a lawyer, by the will of God."

"Ed, a nurse, by the will of God."

"Joyce, a homemaker, by the will of God."

"Randy, a custodian, by the will of God."

Reread: Ephesians 1:2

What greeting did Paul extend to the believers at Ephesus?

Why did he limit his greeting to this group of people?

Here we see peace specifically and purposefully mentioned after grace. What prerequisite is necessary for one to have peace with God? (See Romans 5:1 for help.)

Note: Here and many other places in the New Testament we see Jesus referred to as the "Lord Jesus Christ." We might do well to realize that this phrase communicates His title, His name and His mission in three simple words.

Please explain and expound upon this in your own words.

Reread: Ephesians 1:3

What special privilege does Paul say believers enjoy?

Why is this privilege extended to believers?

How might you define this privilege in concrete and practical terms? Please list the characteristics of this blessing or privilege that come to mind.

1.

2.

3.

4.

5.

6.

7.

This verse also speaks of "every spiritual blessing." Having defined some of the important characteristics of this concept, how might you concisely define it?

After thinking about it, how might you define the spiritual blessings God has given you in everyday terms?

John 5:24

Romans 10:9

Romans 10:13

We see the concept of this antinomy working in John 6:37 where we find that all who come are received and all that are given come.

Some people find it helpful to think of this in terms of a "life parade." Imagine God, who is not bound by the constraints of time, flying in a helicopter high above a parade of the events that will make up your life. He knows the beginning from the end, He knows the way He wants you to go, and yet you have a choice.

Does this concept seem difficult to understand? No wonder.

See:

- Isaiah 55:8-9

- Ephesians 3:18

Reread: Ephesians 1:5

What did God decide in advance for those who come to Him by trusting in Yeshua Ha-Maschiach, the Jewish Messiah, who we know as Jesus?

Let's take a moment and further attempt to make two words about the future, God's foreknowledge and their meaning more clear, drawing upon insights from Warren Wiersbe.

1. The first word is "predestination." As this word is used in the Bible it refers primarily to what God does and will do for people who have come to know Him through a personal relationship with Jesus Christ. <u>Nowhere in the</u>

<u>Judeo Christian Scriptures does it indicate that anyone is predestined to hell. The word is used only in relationship to God's people.</u> For example, God's purpose for history and believers as He has already decided relates to:

- The crucifixion (Acts 4:25-28).

- Our adoption into the family of God (Ephesians 1:5).

- Our conformity to Jesus (Romans 8:29-30).

- Our future inheritance (Ephesians 1:11).

2. The second word is "election," which refers to people, their choices and God's foreknowledge as already discussed.

Reread: Ephesians 1:6

What should be our response to God's action on our behalf through His Son?

Reread: Ephesians 1:7

How did God essentially purchase our freedom?

Why did He do this?

Why was this necessary? (See Romans 3:23 for help.)

Reread: Ephesians 1:8

What three specific things has God showered upon us?

Please make a list.

1.

2.

3.

Note: You may need to review this verse in a few different translations to grasp the fullness of the meaning available.

Read: James 1:5

What must one do to appropriate this shower of powerful benefits?

Note: It is instructive to examine the words translated "wisdom," "prudence" or "understanding" in the original language.

- The word translated "wisdom" is *sophia*. This means knowledge that sees into the heart of things, which knows them as they really are.

- The word translated "prudence" or "understanding" is *phronesis*. This means understanding that leads to right action.

How does this knowledge of the original Greek words impact your understanding of the concept we are discussing in Ephesians 1:8? Please put this in your own words.

Dr. Charles Missler said:

"We are to be sanctified through this truth:

- Christ has given to us the ability to see the great ultimate truths of eternity and thus to properly solve the problems of each moment of time."

Note: Sanctification is the ongoing process of being made Holy as God intended us to be.

What do you think about what Dr. Missler says is available to believers?

Is he right according to what we see in God's Word?

Reread: Ephesians 1:9

What is at the center of God's marvelous plan?

Note: In the original language the word used for "mystery" is *musterion*. This is a sacred secret previously unknown but here revealed. It is of interest that this same word is used a number of other places in the New Testament as other ancient mysteries are revealed to believers. Take a look at the following references where this same word is used and note what we learn from each. Some of these passages are long so they might be relegated to personal inquiry outside of a shorter group discussion.

The Kingdom of Heaven

- Matthew 13:1-50

Iniquity

- 2 Thessalonians 2:7

Babylon

- Revelation 17 and 18

The Church as One Body

- Ephesians 3:1-12

- Romans 16:25

- Ephesians 6:19

The Church as the Bride of Christ

- Ephesians 5:23-32

The In-Dwelling Messiah

- Galatians 2:20

- Colossians 1:26-27

The Fullness of the Godhead

- 1 Corinthians 2:7

- Colossians 2:2

- Colossians 2:9

Godliness

- 1 Timothy 3:16

The Rapture

- 1 Corinthians 15:51-52
- 1 Thessalonians 4:13-17

Israel's Present Blindness

- Romans 11:25

The Will of God

- Ephesians 1:9

The Seven Stars

- Revelation 1:20

Before going on we should also review 1 Corinthians 4:1 where we learn that we are to be stewards of these mysteries.

How do you feel about this responsibility?

Reread: Ephesians 1:10

When will God's plan be accomplished in all its fullness?

Note: A modern heresy is the division of life into the "sacred" and "secular."

Read the following verses and discuss what they have to say about this idea.

Colossians 1:17-20

Hebrews 1:3

Colossians 3:23

D. L. Moody used to warn about people who were "so heavenly minded that they were of no earthly good." How can we guard against this?

Reread: Ephesians 1:11

Why have believers received an inheritance from God?

What is the direct result of this inheritance in the life of a believer whether one realizes it or not? (See Romans 8:28 for a direct expansion of this principle.)

How should knowing that God specifically chose you to be His child and representative impact the way you communicate to others about Him?

Reread: Ephesians 1:12

What was God's purpose in revealing His Word and His Messiah through the Jews?

Why do you think He chose to use this extremely small, frequently oppressed, sometimes slaughtered, and often abused group of people?

Reread: Ephesians 1:13

What two things happened when some of the Gentiles heard the truth?

1.

2.

It is also interesting to see that Ephesians 1:13 rounds out the concept of the Trinity in this passage. We find:

God the Father in Ephesians 1:3.

God the Son in Ephesians 1:7.

God the Holy Spirit in Ephesians 1:13.

Reread: Ephesians 1:13-14

What is the role of the Holy Spirit in the lives of believers?

The concept of the Holy Spirit as God's seal upon believers is an important one. This seal indicates the following interrelated concepts. Please discuss the following references regarding the meaning of a seal and how each relates to you if you are a believer.

A seal indicates:

A completed transaction.

- Jeremiah 32:9-10

- John 17:4

A debt paid in full. (*Tetelestai*)

- Colossians 2:14

- John 19:30

Ownership.

- Jeremiah 32:11-12

- 2 Timothy 2:19

Security.

- Esther 8:8

Intended permanence.

- Daniel 6:17

Authenticity.

- Romans 8:9

A guarantee of preservation.

- Ephesians 4:30

- 1 Corinthians 1:22

- John 6:27

A brand of ownership.

- 1 Corinthians 6:19-20

Note: We should realize that the word translated "guarantee" or "earnest," depending upon which translation you are using, is *arrabon* in the original Greek. This indicates a down payment, pledging that the full amount will be paid. The word was used for this purpose by Phoenician traders. It was also used in reference to a bridegroom's gifts of betrothal to his bride.

How does this information about the original language add to your understanding of this concept? What does it mean to you personally?

What is the purpose of this special function?

How does this work in actual experience? Please give an example.

How do you picture the Father, the Son, and the Holy Spirit at work in your life? (See 1 Peter 1:2-3 for more information.)

Reread: Ephesians 1:14

How does this long sentence at the same time relate to our:

Past?

Present?

Future?

Application Questions

How can you share the blessings God has given you with other people in the days ahead?

What specifically can you do this week to thank God for what He has done for you?

Close in Prayer

What two aspects of Paul's prayer for these people stand out in your mind?

    1.

    2.

Reread: Ephesians 1:17

What two specific things did Paul first ask God to do for the Ephesians?

    1.

    2.

Note:

<u>Revelation</u> or <u>Insight</u> has to do with the imparting of knowledge.

<u>Wisdom</u> has to do with the proper use of knowledge in our lives.

Understanding this differential, how would you describe the interworking of these two concepts in the life of a believer?

Could the insight and wisdom mentioned in Ephesians 1:17 have to do with what is mentioned in Ephesians 1:3? How so?

Why do you think these are the first two things Paul seems to have asked God to give to the Ephesians?

Read:

Isaiah 11:2

1 Corinthians 2:10

John 14:25-26

John 16:12-14

1 John 2:27

2 Timothy 3:16-17

What is the source of all real insight and true wisdom?

Reread: Ephesians 1:18

What did Paul next pray about for the Ephesians?

What does verse 18 say that the impact of this will be?

To whom, in particular, is this privilege extended?

Why do you think this topic was next on the list of things Paul prayed about for these early believers?

Is it necessary for the "gifts" noted in Ephesians 1:17 to become a reality in one's life before the privilege noted in verse 18 can be experienced? How so?

This verse also speaks of believers as the "rich and glorious inheritance" of God. What do you think this means?

Reread: Ephesians 1:19-20

What is the final request we see in Paul's initial prayer for these people?

How might you describe what Paul wants these people to understand in your own words? Please expand and explain.

Why might this be so important to them?

To whom, specifically, is this great resource available?

According to Ephesians 1:19-20, what is the magnitude of this resource?

Reread: Ephesians 1:20

Where is Jesus seated now?

The position of Jesus in relationship to the Father is quite significant. Read the following verses to see what we learn about this location as a place of:

1. Distinction (Hebrews 1:3).

2. Privilege (Hebrews 1:13).

3. Power (Matthew 26:64).

4. Delight (Psalm 16:11).

5. Dominion (1 Peter 3:22).

Please succinctly summarize and list the major points Paul prayed about for the believers in Ephesus:

1.

2.

3.

4.

Reread: Ephesians 1:21

Also read: Colossians 1:16-17

What is the position of Jesus in relation to all powers and authorities?

Please list the powers and authorities mentioned or alluded to over which Jesus Christ is supreme.

1.

2.

3.

4.

5.

6.

7.

Read:

1 John 5:3-5

Ephesians 3:16-18

Believers have the ability to defeat all of these powers by utilizing the tools God has made available. Paul expounds upon this in the sixth chapter of Ephesians.

Reread: Ephesians 1:22

Over what things does Jesus have authority?

Specifically who benefits from the authority that rests in Jesus Christ?

Why then, one might ask, does evil still exist in the world? While books have been written to explain this, the answer is quite simple.

1. Hebrews 2:8 shows us that His headship is not being fully exercised just quite yet.

2. 2 Peter 3:9 tells us that He is giving people time to come to Him before His return.

Reread: Ephesians 1:23

What is the relationship of Jesus Christ to those who trust Him?

Please explain in your own words what you take this to mean.

How far does the presence and authority of Jesus extend?

From what we have studied today, is the power available through Jesus sufficient for your life? How so?

How does the knowledge of His authority make you secure?

Application Question

What do you need to do to make the power available through Jesus Christ a real force in your life this week?

Close in Prayer

BETTER THAN WE DESERVE
EPHESIANS 2:1-10

Open in Prayer

Group Warm-Up Question

When have you shown mercy to a person who deserved to be punished?

Read: Ephesians 2:1-10

Reread: Ephesians 2:1

What one word does Paul use to describe the state of the believers in Ephesus before they trusted Jesus?

What caused them to be in this state?

Do you?

Dr. Charles Missler says "No one else could have done it; no one else would have done it." What do you think about what he said? Do you agree or disagree? Why?

Reread: Ephesians 2:5

What specific thing did God do that gives life to those who trust Jesus?

Reread: Ephesians 2:6

What position has God given believers by virtue of His power?

What do you think this means?

If this is the actual state of believers, and their future is accomplished and secure, what ought to be their involvement with trivial matters of life? Please explain.

Reread: Ephesians 2:7

What will God show in the ages to come?

How does knowing this make you feel?

Reread: Ephesians 2:8

As a result of which of His characteristics did God "save" believers?

When does this take effect in the life of one who makes the decision to trust Jesus?

Who can take credit for this good result?

Why is this true when one must take some action to appropriate God's great gift?

Why is it important that we realize this is a gift?

From what has He saved those who trust in Jesus, Yeshua Hamaschiach, the Jewish Messiah?

Reread: Ephesians 2:9

For what is Salvation a reward?

Who can boast about having their lives changed through a personal relationship with Jesus Christ?

Read: Romans 3:27

About what can a believer boast as it relates to their position with God?

What impact does it have upon listeners when one gives proper credit to Whom it is due?

How does this apply to one's new life as a believer?

Read the following verses to help summarize the plight of human beings and the solution:

Romans 3:23

Romans 6:23

Ephesians 2:8-9

Romans 10:10

Philippians 1:6

Philippians 3:14

2 Corinthians 5:17

Note: One's new life in Jesus, when they find it, is not just a promise to be fulfilled in the future. It is a present reality.

What are your thoughts and feelings about this whole process?

Reread: Ephesians 2:10

How are believers described in this verse?

How does it make you feel to know that God feels this way about you if you have trusted Him through His Son?

How has God done this?

What does He intend to be the result of this change?

Read James 2:14-26 to see the interworking of works and faith.

In today's inquiry we have established that:

1. Humans cannot put themselves right with God through any combination or accumulation of good works.

2. When one is put right with God through Jesus this relationship should be evidenced in one's life.

The motivation for the way in which one's life is lived is changed. Please review the following verses and note what we learn about the life of a believer.

Matthew 5:16

2 Corinthians 9:8

Colossians 1:10

2 Timothy 3:17

Titus 2:14

Hebrews 13:16

When did God plan to make provision for our reconciliation to Him and the good things that follow?

Grace and Mercy

While grace and mercy are related concepts, they are actually vastly different.

Grace: God's favor by which we get what we do not deserve.

God's Mercy: God's restraint by which we do not get what we do deserve.

How would you describe these two concepts in your own words? Please expound and perhaps give an example.

Why doesn't anyone deserve God's grace, mercy and riches?

Application Question

With whom can you share the news of God's grace? How?

Close in Prayer

WEEK 4
THE PRIVILEGE OF ADOPTION
EPHESIANS 2:11-22

Open in Prayer

Group Warm-Up Question

What people have you known whose family connections and upbringing provided them with advantages in life?

Read: Ephesians 2:11-22

Reread: Ephesians 2:11

What did Paul tell the Ephesians to remember?

What were the Gentiles called by the Jews?

Note: At the time Paul wrote this letter Gentiles were despised by the Jews. Referring to someone as "uncircumcised" was an extreme term of derision. Conversely, God made momentous promises to the Jews. Some of these promises were to them as a people and others He purposed to fulfill in a dual sense through the Jewish Messiah. This small group of people would indeed play a major role in the future of all mankind. See:

Genesis 12:3

Isaiah 42:1

Isaiah 42:6

Isaiah 42:9

How did being physically circumcised impact the Jews? Please make a list.

1.

2.

3.

Please read the following verses and note what else we learn about circumcision:

Romans 2:25-29

1 Corinthians 7:19

Galatians 5:6

Galatians 6:15

Philippians 3:2-3

Colossians 2:11

Reread: Ephesians 2:12

What was the predicament in which the Gentiles found themselves prior to becoming believers? Again, please make a list.

1.

2.

3.

4.

5.

Note: The term foreigner as seen in some translations of this verse is the equivalent of Gentile. See Mark 7:24-30 for an illustration of this.

To whom were the promises made that Paul refers to in Ephesians 2:12?

Note: These promises include many things, some of which we have already covered today. The many promises are extensive and to list them all would be beyond the scope of this study on Ephesians. That being said we would do well to realize that they encompass:

1. God's promise of the Messiah to Israel and salvation through the Jews. See:
   • Matthew 15:24

   • John 4:22

2. The subsequent blessings promised to the Gentiles. See:
   • Genesis 12:3

   • Isaiah 11:10

- Isaiah 60:3

3. The interesting, geographically specific, and extensive land promises found throughout the Tanakh, what Jews call the Old Testament. See:
   - Genesis 12:7

   - Genesis 13:15

4. The return of the Jews to the land deeded to them by the Creator. See:
   - Ezekiel 37:21

   - Isaiah 66:7-8

5. The situation in Jerusalem as of this writing. See:
   - Zechariah 12:2-3

Additional Note: In realizing the position of the Jews and Gentiles we should also realize, as mentioned in Ephesians 2:12, no covenants had been made with the Gentiles since the time of Noah.

Reread: Ephesians 2:13
What happened to the Gentiles who placed their faith in Jesus, the Jewish Messiah?

What was it that made this possible?

Reread: Ephesians 2:14

Who was it that brought peace to Jewish and Gentile believers?

How would you describe the characteristics of this peace?

Note: This would have been especially hard for the Jewish believers to participate in without the power of God's Spirit. They had been taught that Gentiles were the source of all corruption, unfaithfulness, debauchery, dishonesty, and evil in the world from the time they were born.

Read:

John 16:33

Acts 10:36

What other insights do these verses give you into the peace brought as a result of a personal relationship with Jesus?

In a forward looking sense the Tanakh also promised an external peace that would ultimately be realized through the Jewish Messiah. See:

Isaiah 9:6

Haggai 2:9

Zechariah 9:10

Reread: Ephesians 2:15-16

How, specifically, did Jesus make peace between Jews and Gentiles? Please list the main points:

1.

2.

3.

4.

As a result of this process, what happened to the hostility between Jews and Gentiles?

Is it necessary for individual Jews and individual Gentiles to both place their trust in Jesus to experience this peace? Please think of examples to support your thoughts about this?

Why do some religious institutions today seem to maintain a wall between themselves and those outside their group even though they may give lip service to the same core beliefs?

How should various groups of people who have found real life in Jesus as referenced in John 10:10 relate to each other? How does this apply to people from different ethnic, racial, and national backgrounds? Please explain.

Note: It is important that we realize the body of believers, which in an all-encompassing sense we call the "Church," is a new creation. It is different from anything that came before and has:

1. A distinct calling.

2. A distinct identity.

3. A distinct destiny.

4. A unique place in the purposes of God.

We must also realize that God similarly has unique and distinct programs as seen in His Word for Israel and the Jews.

While those finding life in Jesus retain their racial and ethnic identities we find some new commonalities. These include:

1. Gentiles and Jews now have equal rights and privileges.

2. Jews and Gentiles are fellow members of the "Body of Christ (the Jewish Messiah)."

3. A Jew, like a Gentile, has the future hope of reigning with the Messiah instead of being a subject in His kingdom.

4. A Jew is no longer under the law in a fashion similar to the Gentiles.

5. National identities of Jews and Gentiles, while of import, are superseded as they jointly become followers of Jesus.

Reread: Ephesians 2:17

What was the position of the Gentiles prior to receiving the Good News of peace available through Jesus?

What was the position of the Jews prior to receiving this Good News?

What commonality characterized both groups?

Note: It may help us to think of taking target practice when considering this question. If a bullseye is the goal, a novice taking their first shot might miss the target entirely. They would be said to be far from the bullseye. An expert marksman would presumably do much better and place his shots closer to the bullseye. However, if neither hits the center of the target they have both failed. Neither one has hit the bullseye, which in terms of our discussion is Yeshua Ha-Maschiach, Jesus Christ, the Jewish Messiah.

Reread: Ephesians 2:18

What is the result of what Jesus has done?

Who, in particular, makes this possible and how does this play out in real life? Please think of an example.

Read: Galatians 5:22-23

How do these verses help in understanding what is happening in Ephesians 2:18?

Reread: Ephesians 2:19

What four things happened to the Gentiles as a result of trusting Jesus? Please make another list:

1.

2.

3.

4.

Reread: Ephesians 2:20-21

Also read:

1 Corinthians 3:11

Psalm 118:22

Acts 4:11

1 Peter 2:4

What seven aspects of the reconciliation between Jews and Gentiles as followers of Jesus can you find in these verses?

1.

2.

3.

4.

5.

6.

Reread: Ephesians 2:22

What three primary points does Paul again drive home in the final verse of today's passage?

1.

2.

3.

Why do you think God repeatedly drives home the role of the Son, the body of believers, and the Holy Spirit in today's passage?

Could it be that as human beings we might tend to forget the role and importance of the primary components of a successful and growing group of believers? How so?

Read Ephesians 2:11-22 once again but very slowly, making note of every time God uses words like one, united, between, reconciled, all, family and together. You may want to consider underlining them in your Bible. Why do you think the Holy Spirit continues to use these interrelated words and concepts as part of this passage?

Application Questions

What can you do to show God's love to someone who is outside of His family this week?

What can both Jewish and Gentile believers do to be sure that we stay on track as we relate to other believers?

Close in Prayer

ANCIENT MYSTERY REVEALED
EPHESIANS 3:1-13

Open in Prayer

Group Warm-Up Question

If you found buried treasure in your backyard, what would be your first course of action?

Read: Ephesians 3:1-13

Reread: Ephesians 3:1

Why was Paul in prison?

Note: We can see that Paul's simple statement in Acts 22:21 led directly to his imprisonment.

Reread: Ephesians 3:2

What did the Ephesians already know about Paul's special task?

Reread: Ephesians 3:3

How was this secret plan revealed to Paul?

Paul noted that he had already written briefly about this mystery. Students of the Scriptures will realize that Jesus Himself as well as Peter also spoke about this. See:

Romans 16:25

Romans 16:26

Colossians 1:26

1 Corinthians 2:7

Matthew 13:10-17

Matthew 13:35

John 10:1-16

1 Peter 1:11-12

Reread: Ephesians 3:4-5

How does Paul say he was able to receive insight into God's special plan?

How did the apostles and prophets receive this same type of knowledge?

What was necessary for the Ephesians to also understand God's plan? There are two ingredients noted. Please list them:

1.

2.

Note: It is interesting to realize that this plan had been revealed by the Old Testament Jewish prophets over thousands of years. It had not, as of yet, been completely understood by the people of the time. As hard as it was for both Jews and Gentiles to grasp these truths then, it is sometimes just as hard for these two groups to grasp them today.

Why is it that Gentiles, without the special empowerment from God's Spirit, often have trouble grasping His plan today as it applies to both them and the Jews?

Why is it that Jews, without the special empowerment from God's Spirit, often have trouble grasping His plan today as it applies to both them and the Gentiles?

This difficulty notwithstanding, there seem to be more Jews and more Gentiles today beginning to understand this mysterious plan of God as it relates to both groups. Why might this be?

Reread: Ephesians 3:6

The secret plan of God as discussed here by Paul has a number of components. Please list them:

1.

2.

3.

4.

5.

6.

Paul had already mentioned this concept as part of his communique to the Ephesians in:

Ephesians 1:10

Ephesians 2:11

Ephesians 2:22

However, he is now explaining the tremendous impact of this "secret." The Gentile believers are now "joint heirs." See:

Ephesians 4:4

Acts 15:8

Galatians 3:14

The Tanakh (what Jews call the Old Testament) predicted that the Gentiles would be blessed through the Jews. See:

Genesis 12:3

Isaiah 11:10

Isaiah 42:6

Isaiah 40:6

Isaiah 55:6-7

Isaiah 60:3

Zechariah 2:11

Malachi 1:11

However, we note that while the Gentiles were predicted to be blessed by the Jews, we do not learn of their joint heirship as fellow members of the body of believers until the first century A.D.

We should also realize that it is predicted that at a future point Israel will be blessed as the head of all nations. See:

Isaiah 60:12

At the same time Gentiles will be blessed through Israel. See:

Isaiah 60:3

Isaiah 61:6

Zechariah 8:23

As we reviewed in an earlier session of the study on Ephesians, Israel and the church have distinct and separate roles in the plan of God. In short:

1. Israel will be blessed under the rule of the Jewish Messiah (Jesus).
   - See Hosea 3:5

2. The Church, made up of Jewish and Gentile believers, will reign with Him over the entire universe.
   - See Ephesians 1:22-23

Reread: Ephesians 3:7

How did Paul receive the task of being instrumental in explaining God's plan?

How did he receive the gift of God's grace?

Paul already mentioned the power available to believers. He also mentions it elsewhere in the letter to the Ephesians. Read the following verses and list what we learn about this power:

Ephesians 1:19-23

Ephesians 3:20

Ephesians 4:16

What we learn about His power:

1.

2.

3.

4.

5.

6.

7.

Note: In the original Greek the word used for "working" is *energeia*, which means "energy." The word used for "power" is *dunamis* which is the root of the English words "dynamite" and "dynamic." What else do we learn about this power from the original language?

Reread: Ephesians 3:8

What was Paul's attitude about how God was using him?

Paul was in prison for his ministry. How could he have possibly regarded his task in explaining God's plan as a privilege when he was suffering so much for doing it? Please explain.

Perhaps we can gain a greater appreciation for Paul's attitude when we revisit a quick summary of his life story. While this can be seen in a number of places through the New Testament, a review of some key passages, primarily from the book of Acts, gives us a good foundation. Please read the following references in narrative form (just read through it as a story) for background:

Acts 8:1-3

Galatians 1:13

Philippians 3:6

Acts 9:1-31

Acts 10:34-48

Acts 13:1-3

Acts 13:16

Acts 13:26-31

Acts 13:44-49

1 Timothy 1:12-15

Read the following verses for a greater understanding of what God was calling Paul to do. Please put each into your own words.

Acts 9:15

Acts 13:47

Acts 22:21

Galatians 2:2

Galatians 2:8

Read: Isaiah 6:5

Also realize that after he became a believer and ultimately an apostle, Saul became known as "Paul." In Greek *Paulus* means "little."

What insight does Isaiah 6:5 and the understanding of the Greek meaning of Paul's name give you into his situation and commission?

We ought to also remember that Paul was a Pharisee and as such a leader of Jewish orthodoxy when he met Jesus. See:

Philippians 3:1-11

Galatians 1:11-24

After he trusted Jesus on a personal basis he displayed greater courage when he defended the unity of the Gentile and Jewish believers, sometimes referred to as "The Church."

Reread: Ephesians 3:9

What was Paul called to disclose?

Why do you think God had not made this plan entirely clear for all to see until this point in human history?

Reread: Ephesians 3:10

What was God's purpose in revealing His plan?

To whom did He particularly want to show His wisdom in all its richness?

How, specifically, would these entities be able to actually see God's plan?

While this may sound a little strange to some "modern" readers, this concept can be seen elsewhere in the Scriptures. We see this referenced in the following verses:

1 Peter 1:10-12

Luke 15:10

1 Corinthians 11:10

1 Corinthians 4:9

What four things do we learn from these excerpts from the Scriptures?

    1.

    2.

    3.

    4.

Reread Ephesian 3:11

For how long had this been God's plan?

How did God carry out His plan?

In Ephesians 3:1-11 God repeatedly makes reference to His special plan in many ways. Please slowly read these verses again and keep a tally of every reference or inference to this plan. What is your final total?

Why do you think the Holy Spirit inspired Paul to do this so many times in this short passage?

Reread: Ephesians 3:12

What is the result of trusting Jesus, the Jewish Messiah in real time?

Why is this such a special privilege?

Read the following verses as you think about your answer:

Hebrews 12:29

Habakkuk 1:13

Psalm 95:3

Jeremiah 23:20

Psalm 93:1

Deuteronomy 6:4

Deuteronomy 32:4

Psalm 18:30

James 1:17

Exodus 3:4-5

Isaiah 6:3

Revelation 4:8

Revelation 1:17

Reread: Ephesians 3:13

Why did Paul tell the Ephesians to not despair?

In what way was Paul suffering for them?

Why should the Ephesians have felt honored and encouraged by Paul's imprisonment and suffering? Please explain.

Do you feel honored or encouraged when believers are discriminated against, attacked, or even tortured to death for their faith today?

Why do you feel this way?

Application Questions

In the days ahead, what can you do to help outsiders feel welcome in your group of believers?

What can you do this week to develop patience and endurance so that you will not be discouraged when suffering comes your way?

Close in Prayer

WEEK 6

POWER
EPHESIANS 3:14-21

Open in Prayer

Group Warm-Up Questions

What makes you feel powerful?

How often do you pray for those you love?

Read: Ephesians 3:14-21

Also Read: Ephesians 3:1-13

Note: In speaking about Paul's letter to the Ephesians Chuck Missler said "Paul is saying, "I want you to get your hands on your wealth, realize how vast it is, and start to use it."" What do you think about Dr. Missler's statement?

55

Reread: Ephesians 3:14

What posture did Paul assume when praying about the mystery he discussed in Ephesians 3:1-13?

Why do you think he assumed such a posture after thinking about this great mystery?

Did he always get in this position when praying? Why or why not?

Do you ever get in this position when praying? If so, when? If not, why?

Is it necessary to always kneel when praying to make it effective?

In Scripture we see:

1. Solomon praying effectively when standing in 1 Kings 8:22.
2. King David praying effectively when sitting in 1 Chronicles 17:16.
3. Jesus praying effectively when bowing to the ground in Matthew 26:39.
4. That the posture of one's soul is most important when praying in John 16:33.

Reread: Ephesians 3:15

What does Paul remind us about the God of the Bible in this verse?

How might this have impacted his posture during his prayer?

Read: John 1:1-4

How was the Word involved with creation?

How do you understand God the Father to have interacted with the Word to bring all things into physical reality?

It is important for us to realize that in Scripture there is no such thing as the "Universal Fatherhood of God" to all peoples effectively "saving" them. Nor, according to the Scriptures, is everyone automatically a child of God. Read the following verses to see what God's Word has to say about this concept:

John 1:11-12

John 3:7

1 John 3:1-2

Now, please put these truths into your own words.

Reread: Ephesians 3:16

What did Paul request of the Father?

What do we learn about the Father's resources in this verse?

What is the result of accessing God's resources?

Please list the two components mentioned.

1.

2.

Through Whom must this be done to be effective?

So far in today's passage we have seen God the Father, His Son and the Holy Spirit mentioned either directly or by inference.

What significance do you attach to the fact that the power spoken of in Ephesians 3:16 seems to be related to the Father, the Word, and the Spirit working together?

Why is this necessary?

To enhance our grasp of how all of this works see:

1. Romans 8:9 to understand that the presence of the Holy Spirit in one's life is evidence of their salvation.

2. Acts 1:8 to understand that it is the Holy Spirit that provides enablement for mature, stable and intelligent believers.

3. Luke 4:1, Luke 4:14 and Acts 10:38 to understand that Jesus acted in the power of the Holy Spirit.

Paul's other recorded prayers from prison may help round out our understanding of this.

In narrative style please read:

Philippians 1:9-11

Colossians 1:9-12

Read 2 Corinthians 4:16 to realize that our bodies, even while we are living and growing, are also in the process of dying. God's Word provides information that helps the inner person grow even while gradually proceeding toward physical death. Scripture figuratively says that the inner man can:

1. See.
   - Read Psalm 119:18.

2. Hear.
   - Read Matthew 13:9.

3. Taste.
   - Read Psalm 34:8.

4. Feel.
   - Read Acts 17:27.

Scripture also tells us figuratively that the inner man must be:

1. Exercised.
   - Read 1 Timothy 4:7-8.

2. Cleansed.
   - Read Psalm 51:7.

3. Washed.
   - Read Ephesians 5:26.

4. Fed.
   - Read Matthew 4:4.

5. Renewed Daily.
    • Read 2 Corinthians 4:16.

Reread: Ephesians 3:17

According to this verse, what happens when a believer accesses God's power through the Holy Spirit? This verse mentions three things. What are they?

1.

2.

3.

According to Ephesians 3:17 there is one more thing that a believer must do to access the power available through God's Spirit. What is it?

Why is this necessary?

How does it work?

We see the concept of being properly and effectively rooted (grounded) throughout the Old and New Testaments. See:

Psalm 1:1-3

Jeremiah 17:5-8

Matthew 7:24-29

In your own words, please describe what it means in a Scriptural sense to be properly rooted or grounded.

In your own words, please also describe the impact upon one's life when they are properly grounded or rooted.

Reread: Ephesians 3:18

What additional power did Paul want the Ephesians to understand?

Why is this important for believers today?

Why do you think the Holy Spirit inspired Paul to speak of God's love in this manner? How does it impact you?

Linguistically the Greek word *prehendere* is translated "comprehend," "understand," or "apprehend" and means "to grasp."

We should also note that most people speak of 3 dimensions in which we live. Surprisingly, Ephesians 3:18 speaks of four. And, speaking of the four dimensions mentioned in this verse we should realize that nothing has been said about the spiritual world.

Interestingly there was a great Jewish scholar by the name of Nachmanides. He was born in Spain in 1194 A.D. and died in Jerusalem in 1270 A.D. From his studies of the Tanakh, what Jews call the Old Testament, he inferred the existence of ten dimensions. (His beginning hypothesis was developed in Genesis 1.) While this is not the time or place for an inquiry into the theory of relativity, hyperspaces or quantum physics, we can at least say that more may exist beyond the normal confines of mere human perception than is generally imagined. We can certainly rest assured that any such information is not news to God. (See John 1:1-3)

Going further, to help us grasp the extent of God's love and power we might look at the original Greek words used in this verse.

The Greek word *platos* is translated breadth or width and suggests "great extent."

The Greek word *mekos* is translated length and seems to actually relate to "length of time."

The Greek word *hupsos* is translated height and here appears to relate to "rank" or "station."

The Greek word *bathos* is translated depth and might otherwise be used to describe the depth of the darkest deepest part of the sea. This would be the "greatest possible depth."

How does your understanding of the Greek impact the concepts we find in Ephesians 3:18?

With this knowledge of the original language, how might you put this verse into your own words?

Reread: Ephesians 3:19

Having understood the power of God's love, what did Paul want to see the Ephesians do next?

Why do you think understanding God's love seems to enhance a person's ability to experience His love? Please give an example?

How fully can a human being understand God's love?

What happens when a person experiences God's love in their life? Please make a list.

1.

2.

3.

4.

5.

6.

7.

Read:

Colossians 2:9

Ephesians 5:18

What insight do these verses give you into an important prerequisite to experience the fullness of God's love?

Reread: Ephesians 3:20

How does Paul begin to close this prayer?

Why does he do so by first giving glory to God?

What does he say God is capable of?

How is God capable of doing this?

What impression does it make upon you when you realize the potential effect of God's mighty power working within a believer?

Reread: Ephesians 3:21

How does Paul say God will receive glory?

How is He glorified in Jesus, the Jewish Messiah?

How is He glorified in the body of believers, both Jew and Gentile, who he refers to corporately as "the church?"

For how long does this glory last?

How does it impact you to realize the everlasting nature of the time attached to this glory?

Application Questions

Reread: Ephesians 3:20-21

How will internalizing the truth of these verses impact your prayer life?

How will internalizing the reality of these verses impact your life on an every-day basis this week?

Close in Prayer

WEEK 7
MANDATE FOR PERFECT UNITY
EPHESIANS 4:1-16

Open in Prayer

Group Warm-Up Questions

What is it that keeps a good sports team or band unified?

What do you consider to be your greatest talent?

Read: Ephesians 4:1-16

Reread: Ephesians 4:1

What did Paul urge the Ephesians to do?

Some people might say this one sentence preface encompasses the whole intent of today's passage. What do you think?

Why do you think God found it necessary and vitally important to be so very specific about unity among believers?

Read: Colossians 1:10

How do the concepts in this verse tie in with Ephesians 4:1? Please explain.

Going forward, we will attempt to dissect the mass of information included in the portion of Scripture we are examining today in order to come away with clear, actionable principles.

Read: Romans 12:1-2

What does God tell us <u>not</u> to do?

What two specific overriding things must we do?

By what transformational action is this accomplished?

What is the ultimate four-part result of this transformation?

1.

2.

3.

4.

Reread: Ephesians 4:2

What five attitudes and actions that foster unity among believers are mentioned in this verse?

1.

2.

3.

4.

5.

Note 1: It is interesting to realize that in the Greek culture humility was thought of as a vice to be practiced only by slaves. Believers are not to be falsely humble or proud in a negative sense. We are to be realistic and honest in our evaluation of ourselves. (See Romans 12:3)

Note 2: The Greek word *praotes* translated "meekness" in the King James translation is rendered "gentleness" in more contemporary translations. Some people have incorrectly equated this with weakness. However, it actually means "power under control;" the opposite of weakness.

Note 3: The word translated "long-suffering" in the King James translation is often rendered "patience" in later versions. It relates to the ability to endure discomfort without fighting back.

Note 4: The word translated "forbearance" in the King James Version is often simply correctly defined using more modern language in later versions and means "lovingly putting up with all that is disagreeable in other people." This concept can also be found and better understood if read in concert with:

- Colossians 3:13

- 2 Timothy 4:2

How well do you get along with other believers?

Reread: Ephesians 4:3

In addition to the four things we found in the previous verse, what four additional complimentary attitudes and actions are implied in Ephesians 4:3?

1.

2.

3.

4.

Reread: Ephesians 4:4-6

These verses provide a list of ten prerequisites that every member of a believing community must understand if those involved are to approach the kind of unity that God desires. Please list them. (You may need to access several translations to get the full flavor of these prerequisites.)

1.

2.

3.

4.

5.

6.

7.

8.

9.

10.

Important aside: Paul did not deal with unity until he had laid an adequate foundation of Scriptural truth. Believers are to be careful that a desire for unity does not partner them with people putting forth destructive and unbiblical teaching that actually destroys community. Read the following excerpts to see warnings against this difficulty:

Romans 16:17-20

2 John 6-11

In Revelation 2:1-7, a communique from Jesus Christ a number of years in the future to the believers in Ephesus, we see that they had to deal (successfully) with just such a problem. They did, however, have other problems noted in Revelation which ultimately led to their downfall.

We will learn more about dealing with such difficulties later in today's session when we look at Ephesians 4:15.

Reread: Ephesians 4:7

Also read: 1 Corinthians 12:13-16

Having understood the prerequisite common understanding for unity, what must each believer also realize?

Why does God give each of us a special gift?

Why should we do our best to understand the gift or gifts God has given each of us on an individual basis?

Why is it equally important to recognize the gifts God has given to other believers with whom we interact?

What is the net impact upon us, other believers, and the shared relationship when believers mutually recognize and appreciate the gifts God has given each one?

What is the net impact upon a group of believers when this type of realization and appreciation is occurring on an ongoing basis?

Every believer has at least one spiritual gift. While such gifts are mentioned a number of places in the New Testament the following references are primary:

1 Corinthians 12:4-11

1 Corinthians 12:27-31

Romans 12:3-8

Ephesians 4:11

Each list is somewhat different and each is complimentary. These gifts, as we see in today's passage, are tools to be utilized in the positive building of the overall community of believers. They are not to be a source of arrogance, but of service.

Reread: Ephesians 4:8-10

Also read: Psalm 68:18

How might you explain this Old Testament prophecy and its fulfillment in Jesus?

Why is it important that we understand this?

What does it have to do with unity among believers?

Reread: Ephesians 4:11

What five specific gifts and roles are mentioned that God has given to the overall worldwide community of believers? Please list them.

1.

2.

3.

4.

5.

By way of explanation:

An Apostle is one sent with a commission as a divinely appointed representative. In the strictest sense they were to have been witnesses to the resurrection. (See Acts 1:15-22; 1 Corinthians 9:1-2.) They were instrumental in laying the foundation. Conversely, a disciple is a follower or learner. In some sense every believer is sent in the same way as an apostle even though we would be more correctly called disciples. (See John 20:21.)

A Prophet does not necessarily make predictive declarations as was so common in the Old Testament. A prophet speaks forth the Word of God for the purpose of encouragement, edification, and consolation. (See Acts 11:28; 1 Corinthians 13:2; Ephesians 3:5, and 1 Corinthians 14:3.)

An Evangelist is a bearer of the Good News especially to those who are lost and have not yet found a full life in Jesus. (See Acts 8:26-40 and Acts 21:8.) While some have the gift of evangelism this is also the pleasant responsibility and privilege of every believer one way or another.

A Pastor has the role of feeding, leading and caring for the group of believers with which they are involved.

A Teacher helps others understand and apply Scriptural truth. In today's text teachers and pastors are mentioned in the same breath. This suggests that they have a dual role. (See Romans 12:7; 1 Corinthians 12:28-29 and, 1 Timothy 3:2.)

Reread: Ephesians 4:12

What is the shared responsibility of those people to whom God had given the specific four gifts and roles mentioned in the previous verse? Please note the two major components of this responsibility.

    1.

    2.

Do you find the Holy Spirit helping you maintain a bond of unity with other believers? How so?

Reread: Ephesians 4:13

What is the result of the continued application of these gifts in concert with God's Word and promise? Again, this is broken down into a number of component parts. Please list them.

1.

2.

3.

4.

How have you benefited from the leadership in the group or groups of believers with which you are associated?

Reread: Ephesians 4:14

From what will believers be inoculated when the gifts mentioned today are properly applied and utilized? Again, God has provided a summarized list for us. Please note below what we are protected against.

1.

2.

3.

Why are human beings in and of themselves so susceptible to being influenced by the things God has provided available protection against?

Reread: Ephesians 4:15

Instead of being misled, what happens to believers when they appropriate the gifts and protection God has provided?

Please give an example of this in operation.

From what we have read today it is obvious that a believer may sometimes need helpful correction. While there is a biblical formula for this, the manner in which it is done is not only important but also speaks to the authenticity or lack thereof in the situation at hand. Ephesians 4:15 addresses the manner in which truth is spoken. Chuck Smith once said "Truth without love is brutality; love without truth is hypocrisy. Truth unites; lies divide. Love unites; selfishness divides."

What do you think about what Chuck Smith said?

Read: Proverbs 27:6

How does this concept relate to speaking the truth in love? Please explain.

Reread: Ephesians 4:15-16

What is the net result of the Holy Spirit's working in a group of believers and the successful application of the gifts we have discussed today? Please make one final victorious list.

1.

2.

3.

4.

5.

6.

7.

8.

What is your personal responsibility in helping to build up the believers around you?

Application Questions

How do you need to show humility, gentleness and patience in dealing with a difficult relationship this week?

What specific action can you take to assist another believer and thereby build up the community of believers this week?

Close in Prayer

CHANGE FOR VICTORY
EPHESIANS 4:17-5:21

Open in Prayer

Group Warm-Up Questions:

Do you prefer wearing old, comfortable clothing or dressy outfits? Why?

How do you feel when you wear a brand new suit or outfit?

What do you do with your worn-out old clothing?

Read: Ephesians 4:17-5:21

Reread: Ephesians 4:17

How is the thinking of the Gentiles, apart from a life-giving relationship with Jesus, summarized in a few words?

Read: James 1:22

Taking this verse into account with Ephesians 4:17, is enjoying a life as a believer a matter of interesting studies and discussions or of a real and vital life well lived? Please explain.

Reread: Ephesians 4:18-19

Also read: Romans 1:18-22

What are some of the characteristics of the ungodly people described as "hopelessly confused?" Please make a list and pay attention to the differentiating nuances.

1.

2.

3.

4.

5.

6.

7.

8.

9.

10.

According to these verses, what role do such people have in closing their minds and hearts?

What is the import of not caring about right and wrong simultaneously?

How is this different and worse than not caring about either what is right or what is wrong alone and separately?

Reread: Ephesians 4:20

How does what the believers in Ephesus were taught about Jesus differ from what they had experienced in a non-believing environment?

Reread: Ephesians 4:21-22

What are those who follow Jesus told to do?

What are the characteristics of the evil nature and old life one leaves when making a decision to follow the Son?

Reread: Ephesians 4:23-24

Also read:

Romans 12:2

2 Corinthians 5:17

What three things must happen in the life of one who has committed themselves to a new and better life in Jesus?

    1.

    2.

    3.

When one becomes a new person as a believer what qualities begin to become evident in one's life?

    1.

    2.

    3.

    4.

    5.

These verses indicate that when a person makes a legitimate decision to follow Jesus, certain things MUST take place. Why are these things mandatory?

If you are a believer, how do you see the new nature spoken of in these verses taking hold in your life?

When one becomes a believer, their entire outlook changes including their values, goals and world-view. Has this happened to you? How so?

Read: John 17:17

By what means does the positive transformation we are discussing today gradually take place?

Reread: Ephesians 4:25-27

What are the first things that a believer must do when allowing God to create a new nature in his or her life? Please list.

1.

2.

3.

Why do you think these particular behaviors appear to be prerequisites to continued growth as a follower of Jesus Christ?

What happens when a person lets anger gain control over them?

Why does God's Word tell believers to not let the sun go down on their anger?

Have you ever let the sun go down on your anger? If so, what was the result?

Reread: Ephesians 4:28

Why do you think it was necessary for Paul to address the question of thievery?

What is God's plan for anyone who was formerly a thief?

Reread: Ephesians 4:29

Also read:

Matthew 12:34

Colossians 4:6

What kind of language are believers admonished to avoid?

Conversely, what are to be the characteristics of the speech of a believer? Please make a list.

　　1.

　　2.

　　3.

What is the impact upon others when one does not follow the admonishment in this verse?

What is the impact upon both believers and non-believers around them when one allows God to help them follow the pattern of good communication that we see in this verse?

How and why does this happen?

Assuming that you are a believer, what old habits have you discarded?

Reread: Ephesians 4:30

What happens when a believer does not allow God to make the positive changes in their life that He desires for them?

Why is it a terrible thing to bring sorrow to the Holy Spirit?

Reread: Ephesians 4:31

What other things need to be surgically removed from the life of a believer? Please make a list.

1.

2.

3.

4.

5.

Note: This verse also serves as an example of why one must not take a single verse of Scripture out of context. The whole of God's Word must be taken into account when understanding His will and intention for our lives. If this verse were to be taken alone, it would appear that anger in and of itself is wrong. However, examining this in light of representative verses from God's Word as a whole reveals:

1. Jesus Himself became angry.
   - Matthew 21:12-13
   - Mark 11:15-18
   - John 2:13-22
   - Mark 3:5

2. God the Father experiences anger.
   - Psalm 7:11

- Psalm 145:8

- Exodus 20:4-6

- 1 Kings 11:9-11

- Psalm 86:15

- Romans 1:18

3. The apostle Paul became angry.
   - Galatians 1:6-9

   - Galatians 5:12

4. Many Old Testament believers became angry.
   - 2 Samuel 12

5. Guidelines to Anger.
   - Proverbs 15:1

   - Proverbs 29:11

   - James 1:19-20

   - Ephesians 4:26

   - Ephesians 5:1-2

Reread: Ephesians 4:32

What specific actions and attitudes must begin to emerge and then characterize the relations between those who have found life in Jesus? Please list them.

1.

2.

3.

Why are these actions and attitudes so important?

Reread: Ephesians 5:1-2

What overriding goal should be in the minds of believers as they go through daily life?

What impact did the sacrifice of Jesus, the Jewish Messiah, have upon God the Father?

What impact does it have upon the Father when we follow the pattern set forth in these two verses?

Reread: Ephesians 5:3-5

Living a victorious and full life as a believer is not a matter of do's and don'ts. That being said, in these verses God's Word tells us that certain behaviors and attitudes are destructive. What particular behaviors and attitudes do we see in these verses that are so harmful? Please list them.

1.

2.

3.

4.

5.

6.

What is it about these particular ways of thought and action that make them so harmful in one's life? Please give this some deep thought as you construct your answer.

According to these verses, what is the net result of indulging in these practices? Does this seem harsh to you? Why or why not?

Reread: Ephesians 5:6

Also read:

Isaiah 5:20

Isaiah 5:21

Why is it that people try to excuse these clearly defined sins and fool others as well as themselves?

What is the result of deceiving others or oneself about these well-defined actions and attitudes?

Reread: Ephesians 5:7-11

Also read:

1 Corinthians 15:33

John 17:14-16

1 John 2:15-17

Should believers avoid intimate friendships with those who habitually engage in the patterns of behavior cataloged in these verses? Why or why not?

What should believers be doing as a nourishing alternative to the practices under discussion in the verses we are considering today?

Reread: Ephesians 5:12-14

Why do you think Scripture says that it is "shameful to even talk about" certain things?

What happens when one concentrates on a subject and makes it the topic of conversation?

How does this impact a person?

Read: Philippians 4:8

Conversely, how does it impact a person who fills their mind and thoughts with these types of things?

These verses seem to say that we have control over our conversation and thoughts. How can we effectively exercise such control? Reread Ephesians 4:23-24 as you construct your answer.

Some psychologists tell us that if you control your mind you can control your world. What do you think of this statement?

What fruit of the Light do you see in your life?

Reread: Ephesians 5:13-14

What happens when light is shone upon destructive behaviors and attitudes?

What exactly does this mean and how does it take place?

Why does this happen?

Who is the ultimate source of this Light?

Reread: Ephesians 5:15-21

These verses provide an overall summary of how a person can enjoy a full life. Conversely, they also provide a descriptive summary of how one can ruin their life. Please make a list of the things one might do and the specific patterns they can follow to ruin their life as mentioned in these verses.

1.

2.

3.

4.

5.

Now, please make a list of the things God's Word assures us will lead to a life worth living. There are at least eight and we should be sure to find all of them.

1.

2.

3.

4.

5.

6.

7.

8.

Read: Galatians 5:22-23

What evidence do you see that your life is controlled by the Holy Spirit?

Application Questions

What can you do this week to make your thoughts, attitudes and actions more consistent with God's Word and the pattern He has established for us?

How can you help others understand that adhering to the positive patterns laid out in God's Word leads to a full, fulfilling and enjoyable life?

Close in Prayer

WEEK 9

FAMILY
EPHESIANS 5:21-33

Open in Prayer

Group Warm-Up Questions

What husband-and-wife team do you admire?

In your view, what one quality or ability sustains a marriage relationship?

Preface

Discord within families, divorce, abuse, unfaithfulness and the resultant hurt and damage seems to have touched almost everyone. One is reminded of Jesus' words when He predicted:

Matthew 24:12

"Sin will be rampant everywhere, and the love of many will grow cold." NLT

Statistics

In the years immediately after World War II 80% of the children in the country grew up in a family with two biological parents who were married to each other.

These statistics began to change dramatically after the Supreme Court outlawed mentioning God and Bible reading in public schools.

By the 1980's less than 50% of the children in the United States could expect to spend their entire childhood in an intact family.

This trend impacts the well-being of children from disrupted families financially too. We find that children from such families are six times more likely to be poor! Furthermore, 22% of one-parent families will experience poverty during childhood for 7 years or more versus 2% in two-parent families.

Impact of Societal Familial Trends

By 1988 the National Center for Health Statistics study of the children of single parent families reported:

1. They were three times more likely to have emotional and behavioral problems.

2. They were more likely to drop out of high school, get pregnant as teenagers, abuse drugs, be in trouble with the law and be involved with physical or sexual abuse.

3. They were less likely to be successful as adults in marriage as well as at work.

4. The teen suicide rate had tripled.

5. Juvenile crime had increased and become more violent.

6. Their already often poor scholastic performance continued to decline.

Going forward we find that fewer than half of adult Americans today feel that sacrifice for others is a positive moral value. The pervasiveness of this attitude results in an all too common adult quest for freedom, independence and choice in relationships. This instability conflicts with a child's need for constancy, security, harmony and permanence in family life. This uncertainty lends itself to an ongoing cycle of disruption. The statistics show that daughters of single parents are:

- 53% more likely to marry as teenagers if they marry at all.

- 111% more likely to have children as teenagers.

- 164% more likely to give birth outside of marriage.

- 92% more likely to dissolve their own marriages.

Dr. Charles Missler says "Each divorce is the death of a small civilization. It inflicts wounds that never heal. Survey after survey demonstrates that Americans are less inclined than they were a generation ago to value sexual fidelity, lifelong marriage, and parenthood as worthwhile goals."

Today's passage deals with the relationship between husbands and wives. In order to put this in proper perspective lets first be sure we are all on the same page in regard to some of the key concepts being discussed. First, let us focus on love. Read 1 Corinthians 13 in its entirety making note of all the characteristics of love you see.

Characteristics of Love in 1 Corinthians 13

1.

2.

3.

4.

5.

6.

7.

8.

9.

10.

11.

12.

13.

14.

15.

16.

17.

18.

19.

20.

This, of course, is only part of the story. In His Word God has provided us with a picture of a great wife. Read Proverbs 31:10-31 and list the characteristics we find.

1.

2.

3.

4.

5.

6.

7.

8.

9.

10.

11.

12.

13.

14.

15.

16.

17.

18.

19.

20.

21.

22.

23.

24.

25.

And now, we come to the passage under consideration today. The previous two passages focused on love and wives. The material we are looking at now has to do with the marital relationship as a whole and most specifically with the duties of a husband.

Read: Ephesians 5:21-33

Reread: Ephesians 5:21

What must both husbands and wives do to make their relationship effective, satisfying and pleasing to God?

Why might the marital relationship not work as well when this particular element is lacking?

Reread: Ephesians 5:22

Also read:

1 Corinthians 11:3

Colossians 3:18

Titus 2:4-5

1 Peter 3:1-2

In what way are wives to relate to their husbands?

For any organization to succeed there must be some sort of operational structure. Why do you think God defined this so clearly for human beings in familial relationships?

Reread: Ephesians 5:23

How are husbands to relate to their wives?

How much and how deeply does Jesus care for His followers?

How much and how deeply is a husband to care for his wife? Please explain.

Note: The husband is called to headship. This is not dictatorship. He is to love, lead, guide, provide, protect and care for his wife.

Reread: Ephesians 5:24

How is the relationship of the body of believers (also called the church) to Jesus an example to wives?

Reread: Ephesians 5:25

How are husbands commanded to love their wives?

In case you missed it, a husband is expected in Ephesians 5:23 and commanded in Ephesians 5:25 to lay down his life for his wife. Knowing this, how would you characterize the depth of love a husband is to have for his wife?

How does a wife generally feel if her husband loves her the way Christ loves the church?

Does a wife generally mind being subject to such a husband who is acting in obedience to God's Word?

Reread: Ephesians 5:26-27

How did the actions of Christ prepare the body of believers for Himself?

How did this take place?

How then, can a husband do the same thing on behalf of his wife?

Read: John 17:17

What role does God's Word play in all of this? Please explain.

Reread: Ephesians 5:28-30

How, in these verses, is the love a husband is to have for his wife described?

In what way is this similar to the fashion in which Jesus cares for the body of believers?

To what extent is the husband to go if he cares for his wife as Christ cares for His church?

This is the third time in this brief passage that, one way or another, husbands are told to be willing to lay down their lives for their wives. Why do you think the Holy Spirit drives this point home so repeatedly? What is so important about it?

Reread: Ephesians 5:31

The bond between a husband and wife is to be greater than the bond between each of them and their family of origin. Why do you think this is a vital ingredient to a happy and successful marriage?

What can happen when either a husband or wife esteems their relationship with their parents above their relationship with their wife?

Reread: Ephesians 5:31-32

Also read:

Genesis 2:24

Matthew 19:4-6

Mark 10:7-9

What mystical thing happens to a man and a woman when they become husband and wife if done according to biblical principles?

How would you describe this oneness in your own words?

What are some of the key characteristics of this oneness?

1.

2.

3.

How does the bond between Christ and the church illustrate the bond that should exist between a husband and wife?

Reread: Ephesians 5:33

How again must a husband relate to his wife?

Why do you think the primary focus of today's passage seems to be the proper way a husband should relate to his wife?

How must a wife relate to her husband?

Note: It is an article of psychology that the primary need of a woman is to be loved. It is likewise the primary need of a man to be respected. Obviously this was true and incorporated into God's Word before the field of psychology developed and recognized it.

Why do marital relationships work out so well when husbands and wives fulfill these basic needs of each other?

The marital relationship is of great import to God. Why is it necessary for Him to be so specific in His Word with both men and women about having successful familial relationships?

How does a healthy marriage between believers bring honor to God?

Final Note: Obviously, everyone isn't married. As good a godly marriage can be, believers who are single are also used by God in wonderful ways.

See: I Corinthians 7:7-9

Application Question

What is something you can do this week to help a believing couple strengthen their marriage?

Close in Prayer

PARENTS AND CHILDREN

EPHESIANS 6:1-4

Open in Prayer

Group Warm-Up Questions

If you could change one thing about your parents, what would it be?

What do you infer about someone who is overtly disobedient to their parents?

Presuppositions: For parents to have the impact God intends upon their children their relationship must first be intact and consistent with His Word. These prerequisites seem to include the principles found in the following verses. Please look them up and discuss why each is important.

1. See Deuteronomy 6:5 regarding the relationship of parents to God.

2. See Ephesians 5:25 regarding a husband's love for his wife.

3. See Ephesians 5:22 regarding a wife's priorities as it relates to her husband.

4. See Ephesians 5:31 regarding the unity of a husband and wife in their relationship and parenting.

Read: Ephesians 6:1-4

Reread: Ephesians 6:1

For what two reasons should children obey their parents?

In what way might obedience to parents be pleasing to God?

Why is obedience to parents pleasing to Him?

Does obedience to parents in any way bring glory to God? How so?

Why should parents pay attention to the natural inclinations of their children?

Reread: Ephesians 6:2-3

Note: The Greek word used here for honor means to revere, prize, and value. It infers giving respect not just based upon merit, but for one's rank. An example sometimes used relates to leaders. One might not always agree with their decision but should still respect their position. Similarly, children of all ages are directed to "honor" their parents in a biblical sense regardless of whether or not their parents "deserve" honor.

Before proceeding please also read Matthew 15:3-9 to see just how seriously God takes honoring one's parents.

Now read:

Exodus 20:12

Deuteronomy 5:16

Proverbs 1:8

Proverbs 30:17

What does it mean to honor your "father and mother?"

What did God promise to those who honor their parents?

Does this promise hold true today? Why or why not?

Note: These ideas about the role of a father are not new. Read Genesis 18:19 to see God's directive to Abraham.

What was Abraham directed to do in relationship to his sons and their families?

What was to be the result of Abraham's obedience?

Going forward, might a father who is overtly not following God's prescription for healthy familial relationships have trouble in other areas of his life?

How and why might this happen? Please explain.

Read:

Romans 1:30

2 Timothy 3:2

In these verses we see disobedience to parents included with other negative behaviors. Why might these things occur together?

Why is it easier for children to obey fair and loving parents than unreasonable and demanding parents?

While we are to honor our parents, such an expectation from God does not include being disobedient to Him. He and His Word supersede parental authority. How is a believer then to respond to improper or ungodly directives from a parent? Read Acts 5:9 before you construct your answer.

We should also realize that people who have suffered under abusive parents and have trusted Jesus can confidently claim the promises of God for themselves as they heal and develop into the kind of people God intends them to be. See:

Jeremiah 29:11

Psalm 68:5

Romans 8:28

Matthew 11:29

1 John 5:14-15

Ezekiel 36:26

Mark 10:27

2 Corinthians 5:17

We would be remiss if we did not touch further upon the topic of abuse of one sort or another. Believers have a special responsibility toward those people who have been abused as well as to the abusers. Read the following verses to get the flavor of this:

Deuteronomy 16:20

Proverbs 31:8-9

Isaiah 1:17

Jeremiah 4:2

Jeremiah 21:12

Hosea 12:6

Amos 5:15

Matthew 5:6

Reread: Ephesians 6:4

Note: Some writers refer to this verse in such a way as to infer that it communicates what God desires for father/child relationships. However, a careful reading of the text reveals that it entails much more. These are not simply good suggestions; they are commands to believing fathers.

What, specifically, does God command fathers not to do?

Why is this so important?

What impact does it have upon a child when they are mistreated by their father in particular?

When have you seen when this negative interaction has taken place? Please give an example.

Conversely, how does God most specifically command fathers to relate to their children?

What are the three key elements of the relationship of a believing father to his children? Please make a list.

1.

2.

3.

What part of this list is the most overriding and crucial?

How can a father be sure that his discipline and instruction are "approved by the Lord?"

What are some specific ways a parent can avoid exasperating his or her children?

Read:

Proverbs 10:1

Proverbs 22:6

Proverbs 23:13-14

Hebrews 12:11

Proverbs 15:32

Proverbs 23:24

What impact does it have upon children when their parents guide and direct them as God intends?

What formula should parents follow to properly assist their children in their development? Fortunately, there is a Book. Please take a look at the following references from this Book to see some primary parts of the model for growth that God has provided in His dealings with us.

Numbers 14:18

Psalm 145:8

Psalm 86:15

Daniel 9:9

Hebrews 12:6-11

John 17:17

Psalm 119:97

Deuteronomy 6:5-7

2 Timothy 3:16-17

Application Questions

What can you do to improve or strengthen your relationship with your parents?

If you have children, how can you avoid exasperating them?

How do you need to nurture healthy family relationships this week?

Close in Prayer

EMPLOYERS AND EMPLOYEES
EPHESIANS 6:5-9

Open in Prayer

Before we begin we should realize:

1. When today's passage was penned over half of the over 100 Million people in the Roman Empire were slaves.

2. The New Testament has more to say about slaves than kings.
   - See 1 Corinthians 1:26.

3. Paul was careful not to confuse the social system in which he operated with the spiritual order within the church.
   - See 1 Corinthians 7:20-24.

4. During the middle ages in Europe it was common for feudal peasants, who are often thought of as existing as virtual slaves, to pay 25% of the fruit of their labor to the landowner with whom they were associated. It is somewhat shocking to realize that in the United States today the effective tax rate for

individuals including federal, state, local, real estate, school, social security, sales, fuel, and Medicare taxes often exceeds 50% of one's gross income.

5. Slavery in many forms is still common in the world.

6. The slavery one thinks of today is often associated with indentured servitude of immigrants, so-called white slavery, and fundamentalist Islamic countries.

7. However, by the standards of peasants in Feudal Europe, many people today who otherwise consider themselves free might be considered economic slaves.

8. With that backdrop in overtly non-slave economies and nations we will then generally apply our study today to employers and employees as the practical equivalent of slaves and slave owners in the first century A.D. in the Roman Empire.

Group Warm-Up Questions

If you lived long ago and had owned slaves, what kind of a slave owner would you have been?

If you were a slave, what would have been the worst part of being considered someone's property?

Read: Ephesians 6:5-9

Reread: Ephesians 6:5

Why did Paul tell slaves to serve their masters with respect and fear?

Why do you think he told slaves to serve their masters sincerely?

Read: 1 Corinthians 4:2

By definition a slave or employer is put in charge of something.

Fiduciary Relationships

The requirement that a believer execute their duties faithfully and sincerely in the interest of those with whom they are involved puts them in the place of a fiduciary. A fiduciary relationship exists when one person places confidence, faith and reliance in another whose aid, advice and protection is sought in some manner. A fiduciary must act at all times for the sole benefit and interests for another to whom such loyalty is owed.

In what way do believing employers and employees have a fiduciary relationship and responsibility to each other?

Reread: Ephesians 6:6-7

What did Paul tell slaves of his day should be characteristic of their work for their masters? Please make a list.

1.

2.

3.

4.

5.

How could slaves benefit from doing the work of their masters?

With what attitude did Paul tell the slaves to serve their masters?

Relating this to today, what characteristics should believers see in their work for their employers?

How do employees today benefit on a personal level, besides a paycheck, by performing their work well?

What does an employer today think about a lazy, unfaithful, or incompetent employee?

Conversely, how might an employer today be influenced by a faithful, honest, competent and hardworking employee who has their employer's interest at heart?

What does an employer today generally think and feel about a bad employee's values and personal beliefs?

Conversely, what opinion might an employer today almost naturally have of the beliefs, values and life of a good and loyal employee?

Might an employer today even be attracted to the lifestyle, habits, values, and beliefs of a good employee? How so? Please give an example.

Reread: Ephesians 6:8

What ultimate reward should employees seek for their good service to their employer?

Why is this motivation so much greater than mere pay or deferred compensation?

Why should this motivation drive the actions and attitudes of all believers in every area of life?

How might this attitude relate to one's life at home?

How might this same attitude relate to one's performance on a committee or a sports team?

Is this attitude one that, when properly applied, will help a person succeed in all areas of life? How so?

Reread: Ephesians 6:9

What does Paul tell slave owners to not do?

In today's purvue, how should employers not relate to employees?

Beyond what not to do, Paul tells slave owners to treat owners the same way he told slaves to act. In practical terms, how then should a believing employer following God's directives in these verses treat employees? Please make a list of specific behaviors that should be evident.

1.

2.

3.

4.

5.

6.

7.

According to these verses, does God favor employees or employers more?

Why are slave owners, slaves, employees and employers all held to the same standard by God?

What is the result of these common standards in actual practice?

What kind of a place is it to work when an employer treats employees according to these principles?

What is it like for an employer when employees act in accordance with God's directives?

On the other hand, what is it like in the workplace when people do not act in accordance with the verses we are considering today?

Please explain how you see treating employees in this fashion influences them.

Going one step further, how does God want believers to treat all people who are in any way subordinate to them? Please give a practical example.

And, how does He want us to act toward those who are over us? Again, please give a practical example.

What importance do you attach to rank or social status?

What importance should you attach to rank or social status?

Can one's rank or social status be used in a positive way that glorifies God? Please explain and give an example from real life.

Dr. Charles Missler says that the worst and most harmful type of slavery is gradual and is prevalent in the world today. He identifies this as being the enslavement of the mind through cultural lies perpetrated in various forms of media and schools. What do you think of what he said?

If Dr. Missler is right about the worst kind of slavery, what is the solution?

Read John 8:36 as you construct your answer.

Application Questions

How can you improve your attitude toward someone you work with? Please be specific.

How can you remember to work with all your heart at whatever you do, as if you were working for the Lord and not men?

Close in Prayer

Week 12

Prepare for All-Out War
Ephesians 6:10-24

Open in Prayer

Group Warm-Up Questions

How do you protect your home from danger?

Do you tend to be a trusting type of person or are you suspicious of other people? Why?

Introduction in Two Parts

1. William Randolph Hearst was born in 1863 and died in 1951. Beginning his career in publishing in 1887 he founded and ran the largest media company in the United States of America. Today the Hearst organization provides all types of media including digital, print and almost any form

one can think of. Their magazine empire is extensive and includes 21 U.S. titles, 19 United Kingdom titles and almost 300 international editions.

As he amassed his publishing empire William Randolph Hearst ran into a cash flow "problem." He had too much money. In order to alleviate this difficult situation he invested a fortune in art treasures from around the world.

At one point in his collecting career he came across a description of some rare and valuable items he felt that he just had to own. He commissioned his agent to search the world and bring these items home so that he could add them to his museum-like holdings.

Mr. Hearst's agent traveled the world for months seeking these treasures to no avail.

Finally, he found them.

They were in William Randolph Hearst's warehouse all along. Had he simply reviewed the list of the treasures he already had he would have been able to enjoy them from the start.

How was Mr. Hearst's situation with these special treasures similar to the situation of those who have trusted Jesus Christ today?

2. The ancient Greeks had a saying that if you wanted peace you had to *parabellum*. Parabellum means to prepare for war.

In what way might this saying relate to believers today?

Read: Ephesians 6:10-24
Reread: Ephesians 6:10

What was Paul's final exhortation to the Ephesians?

Ephesians 6:10 is demonstrably the Word of God and carries incalculable weight. Do you view this verse as a suggestion to believers today or a command? How so?

Note: The word in the original language for "mighty" is *kratei*, which means "power that overcomes resistance."

What insight do you gain from this knowledge?

Read:

Isaiah 59:16-17

2 Corinthians 10:3-4

It is interesting to see that God uses idioms similar to the ones in today's passage other places in Scripture. Please list the commonalities that you see.

What clues to our victory in the spiritual battle in which we are all engaged do you find in these verses?

Reread: Ephesians 6:11

What did Paul tell the believers to put on?

What portion of these accoutrements are believers to utilize?

What does God's Word promise as a result for believers who do what God tells them to in this verse?

Reread: Ephesians 6:11-12

Who are we not fighting against?

There are, however, a number of entities mentioned with which believers are at war. Please list them.

1.

2.

3.

4.

When are believers at war with the adversaries listed in these verses?

Note: The Greek word used for the schemes, tricks and tactics of the enemy is *methodeias*. This word is used only twice in the New Testament. Read Ephesians 4:14 to see the other usage of this word and to gain a greater understanding of its meaning. Based upon a reading of Ephesians 6:17 and Ephesians 4:14 in concert, how might you describe what we are to expect from our adversary?

Read the following verses and note what else we learn about our enemy.

Ephesians 4:27

2 Corinthians 4:4

1 John 4:4

Revelation 12:9

The unseen world sometimes seems foreign to people in "modern" cultures where people have often become insensitive to anything that is not material. However, as the Scriptures tell us and science confirms, the battle in which we are engaged is taking place on more than simply the physical plane. Read 2 Kings 6:8-17 to see an example of this recorded in the most accurate and authenticated book available.

What do we learn from this passage? Please enumerate.

1.

2.

3.

4.

5.

6.

7.

What do you think you would find if you could press a button and view the unseen battle taking place around you today?

Reread: Ephesians 6:13

How much of the Armor of God are believers instructed to put on?

What is the promised result of properly preparing for battle?

You may have noticed that this is already the second time God makes these points in this short passage. Why do you think He emphasizes this crucial strategic imperative as well as the result in this fashion?

Comment: Notice how this is working. In His Word God is using principles of communication that humans have codified and utilized over time for effective transmission of ideas and concepts. Toastmaster's International says that when you are giving a speech and want to get a point across you do it in three distinct parts.

1. First, you tell your audience what you are going to tell them.

2. Then, you tell them what you said you were going to tell them.

3. And finally, you tell them what you just told them.

While this may seem simplistic it is also extremely effective in getting one's point across in all types of situations. It should not surprise us to see this technique exhibited in God's Word, which is the source of all truth. (John 17:17)

Reexamining today's passage in light of this reveals the pattern that Toastmasters and others have finally figured out. We see:

1. The admonition to put on all of God's armor in verse Ephesians 6:11.

2. The command to use all of God's armor in Ephesians 6:13.

3. The very practical description of exactly how to do this effectively in Ephesians 6:14-18.

Reread: Ephesians 6:14

What are we again told to do in this verse?

Note: This is yet another time we have been told about standing strong and firm in today's short passage. We see:

- Be strong in Ephesians 6:10.

- Put on all God's armor in Ephesians 6:11.

- You will be able to stand firm in Ephesians 6:11.

- Use every piece of God's armor in Ephesians 6:13.

- You will still be standing firm in Ephesians 6:13.

- Truth and righteousness in particular go hand in hand with your ability to stand your ground in Ephesians 6:14.

How do you think the United States of America would be different today if believers had, as a group, seriously followed the admonishments in the first five verses in today's passage beginning in about 1960?

What role does the Holy Spirit play in our ability to stand strong?

What two specific pieces of armor are believers instructed to put on in this verse?

To better understand this verse we should examine the function of these two pieces of equipment at the time in which this letter was written. Paul had a perfect example right in front of him as he wrote about this concept since he was chained to what is presumed to have been a member of the Praetorian Guard. We see other references to Paul's imprisonment in:

- Acts 28:16.
- Acts 28:20.

The Importance of Truth

Dr. Charles Missler says "....truth is *our most precious treasure* (italics are his) to be coveted. Truth is the key to success, fulfillment, victory, or achieving any worthwhile goal. The pursuit of truth is our greatest challenge in every one of our endeavors."

What do you think about what Chuck said regarding truth?

The Sturdy Belt of Truth

The "sturdy belt of truth" is the literary equivalent of the belt worn by a Roman soldier. This belt was between six and eight inches wide. All of a soldier's body armor and combat equipment was attached to it. This secure arrangement gave the soldier freedom of movement when in battle. He didn't have to worry about his armor falling off if it was attached to this sturdy belt.

We should also note that there was a sort of leather apron with small brass plates hanging down from the front of this belt to guard the lower abdomen and groin area, protecting some of the most vulnerable parts of a soldier's body.

Read the following verses to get a better perspective on the concept of the belt of truth as it relates to the Scriptures

John 17:17

John 14:6

Isaiah 11:5

Psalms 51:6

How might you summarize what you learn about the belt of truth in these verses?

Like the Roman belt and its apron of brass plates, why is it so important that believers are protected by truth?

What important vulnerable areas of a believer are being protected by the belt of truth?

Why is the inerrant Word of God so important in holding the whole armor of God together in the life of a believer?

How exactly does this work?

The Body Armor or Breastplate of Righteousness

The Roman body armor referred to in this passage was made of bronze backed with leather. The breastplate protected the vital organs necessary for life. Besides covering the lungs, kidneys, stomach and pancreas, this part of a soldier's armor covered his heart.

Reread: Isaiah 11:5

How are the concepts of truth and righteousness combined in this figurative protective equipment?

Read the following verses and note what we learn about the breastplate of righteousness that every believer must have to be victorious.

Romans 6:13

Romans 14:17

Isaiah 59:17

James 4:7

Psalm 7:3-5

1 Corinthians 4:2 (Yes, this is the right verse.)

2 Corinthians 5:21

1 Thessalonians 5:8

If a Roman soldier failed to wear his breastplate an enemy arrow could easily pierce his heart with fatal results. How does this relate to the breastplate of righteousness that believers are commanded to wear?

What happens in the life of a believer if they fail to put on the breastplate of righteousness? Please give an example.

Reread: Ephesians 6:15

How does this verse say we are to equip ourselves?

The Footwear of the Roman Soldier

This part of a soldier's gear was made of thick leather studded through the soles with hobnails. Part and parcel with these shoes were the greaves. These were protective plates made of brass or other metal covering the shin and in the case of the Praetorian Guards extending up over the knees. This leg armor had been in use in the ancient world for centuries. See 1 Samuel 17:6.

Proper footwear was essential to the Roman soldier for several reasons.

1. These men often had to march long distances requiring great endurance and could not do so without proper protective shoes.

2. Broken footwear could actually render a soldier unable to effectively engage in battle. See Isaiah 5:27.

3. Enemies of the Romans would often employ gall-traps and sharp sticks to block the way of the marching legions. (The punji stick traps employed in Vietnam were merely an adoption of an old invention.) Good footwear and greaves provided protection against these devices.

4. Sturdy footwear enabled a soldier to stand firm in battle.

5. If a soldier lost his footing in battle and slipped or went down it was often fatal. The first slip was often the last.

On the Offensive

One final note about the shoes to be put on is that they are to be donned in preparation for an offensive into enemy territory. This is not a defensive maneuver. We are to move forward as we engage the enemy and offer them the full life available through the Jewish Messiah.

The Good News

Read:

Isaiah 52:7

John 16:33

Note: The prophecy from Isaiah about the peace and salvation that God has made available was written approximately 700 years before Jesus was born.

Second note: The Good News of inner-peace and one's <u>assurance</u> of salvation again refers us back to God's Word and the preeminence of Scripture in the life of a victorious believer.

Why do you think God again refers us back to His Word in Ephesians 4:15? After all, we just read about it in the previous verses.

Reread: Ephesians 6:16

What does Paul say believers will need in every battle?

The Shield of Faith

The Roman shield was constructed of wood and was four feet tall and approximately 2.5 feet wide. The wood was overlaid with leather and linen to absorb fiery arrows. Iron rims were fitted along the top and bottom edges of the shield and an iron circle in the center gave further protection to the hand of the soldier holding the shield on the other side. The integrity of a soldier's shield was essential in battle.

An interesting point of history is that shields in the ancient world could be used by a group of soldiers in combination. In the case of the Romans they sometimes utilized a formation called a "tortoise." In this maneuver 27 soldiers operated in unison with six in the front row and seven in each of the next three rows. With their shields held together over and around them they formed something of a "walking tank." This "tank" was almost impervious to hurtled stones, arrows, spears and the like. In fact, the Romans training in this formation were tested by running chariots over it. One can see an excellent enactment of this formation in the opening scenes of the well-done movie *Risen*.

Faith can be defined as trust based upon fact. For a believer this equates to a firm confidence in the Word of God.

This confidence in the Word of God is well founded. As anyone who diligently inquires has discovered, the Bible is made up of 66 books written by over 40 authors over thousands of years. Every detail is there by design. This amazing book is demonstrably of supernatural origin and engineering. Besides being completely accurate on an historical basis it contains the Words of life available for the asking. Every archaeological find, all work in linguistics, and all of the sciences simply confirm the authenticity and reliability of God's Word as they "advance." Any apparent contradictions with these human fields of endeavor are eventually cleared up with further scholarship when one realizes that the Word of God was right all along. Humanly limited scientists just have to catch up with the facts.

If a believer has any questions about the integrity of the Scriptures as a basis for their life, the time to clear up such concerns is now, before the battle heats up. If a Roman soldier needed to repair his shield it was an immediate life threatening concern and he attended to it without delay. Believers today need to exhibit the same diligence and motivation.

Read: John 14:26

What role does the Holy Spirit play in our shield of faith?

Ephesians 6:16 verse speaks of stopping the fiery arrows aimed at believers by Satan. While this imagery may sound strange at first we can come to understand it if we examine human emotions and their impact upon us.

This concept was brought home to me just this morning as my wife and I were talking. Tragically, our son died last week and Sally said she felt as if a fiery arrow had pierced her heart and she couldn't get it out. She felt as if she were immobilized on a permanent basis. We discussed this in light of the reality of the Scriptures and prayed together. Trust in Jesus Christ, the power of the Holy Spirit and the truth of God's Word helped us pull out the "arrow" of negative, deceptive emotions and thought. This is not a simplistic answer to grief. There will be more "arrows" to be deflected and extracted. But we do have the shield provided by God as we experience victory even in the heat of battle.

What are some of the fiery arrows from Satan that you have had to deal with in your life as a believer?

What are some of the fiery arrows shot by Satan at believers in the ongoing battle in which we are engaged? Please make a list.

1.

2.

3.

4.

5.

6.

This does, of course, bring up a point we have already touched upon. In hand-to-hand battle, shields can become damaged. What did a good soldier do in the first century A.D. when his shield became damaged? He fixed it. What must believers do today when their shields are in some way damaged?

When must believers fix their shields of faith?

How do Bible study, research, prayer, the Holy Spirit, and the relationship one has with other believers play into the maintenance of one's shield as we engage in continual battle?

In our initial information about the Roman shield we also discussed the tortoise formation. In what way must believers act in the same manner as this maneuver as they support each other? Please explain.

If one believer in a group is suffering from some sort of assault from the enemy is it likely that another has already overcome such an assault? How does this benefit the group as a whole? Read Galatians 6:2 as you put together your answer.

Reread: Ephesians 6:17

What two portions of the armor of God are we instructed to put on in this verse?

Helmet of Salvation

The Roman helmet in the first century A.D. was made of bronze or iron. It had two cheek pieces that protected the sides of the soldier's face as well as a plume of horsehair on top. For comfort many soldiers lined their helmet with felt or sponges from the Mediterranean Sea.

Obviously, the helmet protected the head of the soldier. Interestingly, such physiological protection of this vital area also gives one a sort of psychological and emotional assurance. Anyone who has played American football, ice hockey, polo, or engaged in the sport of wrestling has experienced this phenomenon even if they did not realize what was happening at the time.

If you have engaged in an activity that required a helmet, how did it impact you when you put it on and took it off? Please explain.

On a spiritual basis the Helmet of Salvation is even more important.

It is critical to success in the daily battle in which believers are engaged that they are certain of:

1. Their position in relationship to God.

2. Their own salvation.

3. The authenticity of God's Word.

4. God's ultimate victory over evil.

5. Jesus' sacrificial death on the cross.

6. His resurrection.

7. Their assurance of eternal life.

Read the following verses, perhaps in several translations for help as we consider the importance of knowing that our helmet of salvation is secure:

Isaiah 49:23

John 3:16

Ephesians 2:8-9

Romans 8:28-39

Hebrews 7:25

Romans 10:10

Romans 10:11

Ephesians 1:13

1 Corinthians 15:1-4

2 Corinthians 5:17

1 Thessalonians 5:8

2 Timothy 1:12

1 Peter 2:6

How are we assured of our salvation?

What part does God's Word play in our assurance?

What role does the Holy Spirit play in our assurance?

The Sword of the Spirit

The Roman sword, called a *machira,* was one of the most revolutionary developments in weaponry and warfare. (*Machiria* is the word used for this weapon in Greek. The Latin term, with which most people are familiar, is *gladius.*) These weapons were about 24 inches long and honed to a fine edge on both sides. This innovation, when properly used, enabled the Romans to achieve great victories.

Prior to that time swords were normally much longer and sharpened only on one edge. These typical swords of the day were wielded with a cocked arm and were effective when used with a chopping motion as well as a stabbing motion.

With the double edged Roman sword a soldier could duck, weave, and evade an enemy sword stoke and then immediately counter attack when his enemy was off balance with a sword thrust or cut with his vicious razor sharp weapon from any position.

That being said, this innovative weapon required specialized training in its proper use. When one trained with this weapon and practiced on a daily basis he was a formidable opponent to most any foe in close quarters combat.

How is the Sword of the Spirit defined?

How does the necessary daily familiarity and use of the Roman sword, which is crucial for victory, equate to a believer's relationship to Scripture?

Over the course of the past 100 years there have been many experts in the field of weapons and their use. Perhaps the greatest living expert on firearms today is my friend, J.D. Jones. J.D., who himself has been a prolific writer, was also acquainted with a man by the name of Jeff Cooper, the author of *Principles of Personal Defense,* who has been quoted more often than most anyone on the topic. He said:

"Owning a handgun doesn't make you armed, any more than owning a guitar makes you a musician."

"Safety is something that happens between your ears, not something you hold in your hand."

"The only acceptable response to the threat of lethal violence is an immediate and savage counterattack. If you resist, you might just get killed. If you don't resist, you almost certainly will get killed. It is a tough choice, but there is only one right answer."

How might Jeff Cooper's quotes relate to the ownership, practice and use of our primary offensive and defensive weapon, God's Word? Please explain.

It is interesting to see God's Word referred to as "The Sword of the Spirit."

Read the following verses and discuss what you think this might mean and just how it works.

Psalm 119:11

Hebrews 4:12

We should also realize that Jesus Christ Himself used Scripture as a defensive and offensive weapon.

Read Matthew 4:1-11 to see just how He did this.

Note His specific utilization of the concepts in:

Deuteronomy 8:3

Psalm 91:11-12

Deuteronomy 6:16

Deuteronomy 6:13

Isaiah 41:10

Joshua 1:9

John 14:26

In your own words, how is the Holy Spirit involved in the use of God's Word? Please explain in detail and give a personal example.

Important Note: Some people make the mistake of thinking that the Sword of the Spirit is the only offensive weapon mentioned in this passage. We must, however, realize that all portions of a believer's armor enable one to be both on the defense and offense at the same time as they take the message of the Gospel to the world on all fronts.

How do you envision this happening as a practical matter in various walks of life?

Reread: Ephesians 6:18

What are we next instructed to do. Please make a list.

1.

2.

3.

4.

5.

Are we to do this before, during, or after battle?

In today's discussion we already referenced Jeff Cooper, one of the patron saints of self-defense and situational awareness. He developed a color system to quickly and easily delineate appropriate situations of readiness. This system is widely known and followed by security experts around the world. In his system a condition of readiness at any point in time is designated by a color, which relates to one's preparation to act. Interestingly, he also tied this in with one's expected heart rate at these times. It looks like this:

Condition White: In Condition White one is not alert. They are totally unaware of their surroundings and unable to react to any danger. They are completely relaxed, unaware and unprepared. The heart rate of someone in this state is assumed to be 60-80 beats per minute.

Condition Yellow: In Condition Yellow one is relaxed, but alert. They are aware and recognize that a threat or problem might possibly exist. Their heart rate is expected to be in the range of 60-80 beats per minute.

Condition Orange: In this condition one is aware of a specific situation about which they need to be alert. They are aware and focused on a specific identified threat. They know what event or type of action on the part of the threat would act as a "trigger" to make them act. At the same time that one is on alert to a specific threat they are still to pay attention to the surrounding environment. One's heartbeat at this time generally starts to rise to 80-115 beats per minute.

Condition Red: In this condition one is ready to act immediately. They are aware of a specific threat and prepared to go into action right away if the type of "trigger" referenced in Condition Orange is tripped. One's heartbeat at this point is expected to rise to 115-175 beats per minute.

How might these color codes of situational awareness apply to the life of a believer who has donned the full armor of God? Please give an example.

Surprisingly, there is a tendency among some to minimize the importance of prayer in contrast to overt material assistance and physical action. According to Ephesians 6:18 and Scripture as a whole, this is wrong. The two work together. It is through Scripture that we get a correct view of this. It has been said that:

"Bible reading and action without prayer is tantamount to atheism, and prayer without Bible reading and action is presumptuous."

What do you think about this statement?

Believers must realize the vital importance of prayer in the ongoing battle for God. In particular, we should recognize and be thankful for those serving in the role of "prayer warriors."

Heavy Artillery

Note: One cannot overstate the power and necessity of prayer. Chuck Missler likens it to the heavy artillery in a battle. In the days of the Romans this might have been catapults and similar weapons. On the battlefields of today it might involve howitzers with explosive projectiles or depleted uranium shells to penetrate the armor of the enemy.

There are some people whose physical infirmity prevents them from being one of the ground troops in the constant battle in which believers are engaged. However, these same people can act as the heavy artillery in the conflict and are sometimes called "prayer warriors." Their contribution is vital.

Suggested assignment: Have a member of the group agree to view and report on the movie, The War Room at a future session.

Alternatively, the group may wish to schedule in an evening together where they enjoy each other's company, have some snacks, view the movie and discuss it together.

Reread: Ephesians 6:19

What did Paul ask the Ephesians to do for him?

What specifically did he ask them to pray for?

Why do you think that Paul, with all of his experience at speaking, intelligence and apparent inherent willingness to fight for God's truth is asking them to pray for him to be bold?

If Paul wanted prayer support to speak boldly as he should, what do we need?

How can we access this support?

What is the secret plan that Paul is explaining for which he wants the support of the "heavy artillery" of prayer?

A number of years ago Zola Levitt published a book entitled *How Can a Gentile be Saved?* He was making the point that many in today's world have forgotten that Gentiles who come to know Jesus, the Jewish Messiah, in fact have the Jews to thank for their role as His Chosen People in bringing His Word to the world. Indeed, during the first two centuries after the birth of Jesus, those in the powerful Parthian empire regarded Christianity as a more vital sect of Judaism. How are we benefited from realizing that what we call "Christianity" is actually "True Judaism" at its heart?

Reread: Ephesians 6:20

For what, specifically, did Paul say he was in chains?

Although he was in chains, what was his greatest wish?

Read the following verses to get a better idea of Paul's position at this point in his life:

Acts 28:20

Ephesians 3:1

Ephesians 4:1

Philippians 1:7

Philippians 1:13-14

Colossians 4:3

Colossians 4:18

Philemon 1:1

Philemon 1:9-10

Philemon 1:13

What are your feelings and thoughts when you realize that some of the greatest literature of all time was written by Paul, perhaps the most educated and intelligent man of his day, when he was in prison for sharing the Good News of the life available through the Jewish Messiah?

For what does Paul again request the "heavy artillery" of prayer support?

Are people today sometimes in figurative if not literal chains of this nature? How so?

How can believers "in chains" of any sort today learn from Paul's situation and go on to victory?

Focus for Victory

In the verses we have so far examined today we have seen repeated references and allusions to certain aspects of our readiness for success in battle. Notably they have included:

1. God's Word in Ephesians 6:14.

2. The Holy Spirit in Ephesians 6:14.

3. God's Word in Ephesians 6:15.

4. God's Word in Ephesians 6:16.

5. The Holy Spirit in Ephesians 6:16.

6. God's Word in Ephesians 6:17.

7. God's Word in Ephesians 6:17 yet again.

8. The Holy Spirit in Ephesians 6:17.

9. God's Word in Ephesians 6:18.

10. The Holy Spirit in Ephesians 6:18.

11. Prayer in Ephesians 6:18.

12. Prayer in Ephesians 6:18 again.

13. The Holy Spirit in Ephesians 6:19.

14. Prayer in Ephesians 6:19.

15. Prayer in Ephesians 6:20.

16. The Holy Spirit in Ephesians 6:23.

How often do you pray for other followers of Jesus Christ?

How does it impact you when you pray for others?

Reread: Ephesians 6:21-22

How did Paul describe Tychicus?

Note: This is not the only mention of Tychicus in the New Testament. Please read the following verses and note what else we learn about this faithful man.

Acts 20:1-4

Titus 3:12

2 Timothy 4:10-12

What did Paul want Tychicus to do when he went to Ephesus?

How could Tychicus have possibly had a positive impact on the Ephesians when Paul was in chains?

Reread: Ephesians 6:23

What did Paul wish for the believers in Ephesus?

What was to be the source of these good things?

Reread: Ephesians 6:24

Upon whom did Paul wish God's grace to rest?

En sphtharisia in the Greek is translated as the "sincerity" of those who "love our Lord Jesus Christ with an undying love." The literal meaning of the original language includes the concepts of incorruptibility and immortality. The clear meaning is that the love of believers for their Lord is to be pure and without corruption of wrong motives or secret disloyalties. We see these same allusions to immortality and incorruptibility in:

Romans 2:7

1 Corinthians 15:42

1 Corinthians 15:50

1 Corinthians 15:53-54

2 Timothy 1:10

What insights do you gain from this understanding of the original language in concert with these other references?

How does this relate to believers today?

How is this instructive to believers today?

Read: Revelation 2:4

On a sad note, the group of believers in Ephesus did not, as a group, respond properly to the instructions and power laid out so clearly before them in this book of the Bible. How can we be sure to respond properly to God's clear plan for our lives today?

Application Questions

Please inventory your personal armor as discussed in this session. What pieces, if any, either need refurbishing or are missing?

If you have identified any pieces of armor that need attention, what specifically will you do to rectify the situation and prepare for battle?

What can you do to help other believers prepare for battle?

Close in Prayer

Appendix 1

How to Avoid Error
(Partially excerpted from *The Road to Holocaust* by Hal Lindsey)

1. The most important single principle in determining the true meaning of any doctrine of our faith is that we start with the clear statements of the Scriptures that specifically apply to it, and use those to interpret the parables, allegories and obscure passages. This allows Scripture to interpret Scripture. The Dominionists (and others seeking to bend Scripture to suit their purposes) frequently reverse this order, seeking to interpret the clear passages using obscure passages, parables and allegories.

2. The second most important principle is to consistently interpret by the literal, grammatical, historical method. This means the following:

   1. Each word should be interpreted in light of its normal, ordinary usage that was accepted in the times in which it was written.

   2. Each sentence should be interpreted according to the rules of grammar and syntax normally accepted when the document was written.

   3. Each passage should also be interpreted in light of its historical and cultural environment.

Most false doctrines and heresy of Church history can be traced to a failure to adhere to these principles. Church history is filled with examples of disasters and wrecked lives wrought by men failing to base their doctrine, faith, and practice upon these two principles.

The Reformation, more than anything else, was caused by an embracing of the literal, grammatical, and historical method of interpretation, and a discarding of the allegorical method. The allegorical system had veiled the Church's understanding of many vital truths for nearly a thousand years.

Note 1: It is important to note that this is how Jesus interpreted Scripture. He interpreted literally, grammatically, and recognized double reference in prophecy.

Note 2: It is likewise important that we view Scripture as a whole. Everything we read in God's Word is part of a cohesive, consistent, integrated message system. Every part of Scripture fits in perfectly with the whole of Scripture if we read, understand, and study it properly.

Note 3: Remember to appropriate the power of The Holy Spirit.

Read: Luke 11: 11-12   Read: 1 Timothy 4: 15-16

Read: Luke 24: 49   Read: 2 Peter 2: 1

Read: John 7: 39   Read: Mark 13: 22

Read: John 14: 14-17, 26

APPENDIX 2

UNDERSTANDING COMPOSITE PROBABILITY AND APPLYING IT TO THE JUDEO-CHRISTIAN SCRIPTURES

To better understand one of the ways the Creator of the Universe has validated His Word and the work and person of Jesus Christ, it is helpful to get a grasp on composite probability theory and its application to the Judeo-Christian Scriptures.

We are indebted to Peter W. Stoner, past chairman of the Department of Mathematics and Astronomy at Pasadena City College as well as to Dr. Robert C. Newman with his Ph.D. in astrophysics from Cornell University for the initial statistical work on this topic. Their joint efforts on composite probability theory were first published in the book *Science Speaks*.

Composite Probability Theory

If something has a 1 in 10 chance of occurring, that is easy for us to understand. It means that 10 percent of the time, the event will happen. However, when we calculate the probability of several different events occurring at the same time, the odds of that happening increase exponentially. This is the basic premise behind composite probability theory.

If two events have a 1 in 10 chance of happening, the chance that both of these events will occur is 1 in 10 x 10, or 1 in 100. To show this numerically this probability would be 1 in 10^2, with the superscript indicating how many tens are being multiplied. If we have 10^3, it means that we have a number of 1000. Thus 10^4 is equivalent to 10,000 and so on. This is referred to 10 to the first power, 10 to the second power, 10 to the third power, and so on.

For example, let's assume that there are ten people in a room. If one of the ten is left handed and one of the ten has red hair; the probability that any one person in the room will be left handed and have red hair is one in one hundred.

We can apply this model to the prophecy revealed in the Bible to figure out the mathematical chances of Jesus' birth, life and death, in addition to many other events occurring in the New Testament by chance. To demonstrate this, we will consider eight prophecies about Jesus and assign a probability of them occurring individually by chance. To eliminate any disagreement, we will be much more limiting than is necessary. Furthermore, we will use the prophecies that are arguably the most unlikely to be fulfilled by chance. I think you will agree that in doing so, we are severely handicapping ourselves.

The first prophecy from Micah 5: 2 says, "But you, O Bethlehem Ephrathah, are only a small village in Judah. Yet a ruler of Israel will come from you, one whose origins are from the distant past." (NLT) This prophecy tells us that the Messiah will be born in Bethlehem. What is the chance of that actually occurring? As we consider this, we also have to ask: What is the probability that anyone in the history of the world might be born in this obscure town? When we take into account all of the people who ever lived, this might conservatively be 1 in 200,000.

Let's move on to the second prophecy in Zechariah 9: 9: "Rejoice greatly, O people of Zion! Shout in triumph, O people of Jerusalem! Look, your king is coming to you. He is righteous and victorious, yet he is humble, riding on a donkey---even on a donkey's colt" (NLT). For our purposes, we can assume the chance that the

Messiah (the king) riding into Jerusalem on a donkey might be 1 in 100. But, really, how many kings in the history of the world have actually done this?

The third prophecy is from Zechariah 11: 12: "I said to them, 'If you like, give me my wages, whatever I am worth; but only if you want to.' So they counted out for my wages thirty pieces of silver" (NLT). What is the chance that someone would be betrayed and the price of that betrayal would be thirty pieces of silver? For our purposes, let's assume the chance that anyone in the history of the world would be betrayed for thirty pieces of silver might be 1 in 1,000.

The fourth prophecy comes from Zechariah 11: 13: "And the Lord said to me, 'Throw it to the potter'---this magnificent sum at which they valued me! So I took the thirty coins and threw them to the potter in the Temple of the Lord" (NLT). Now we need to consider what the chances would be that a temple and a potter would be involved in someone's betrayal. For our statistical model, let's assume this is 1 in 100,000.

The fifth prophecy in Zechariah 13: 6 reads: "And one shall say unto him, What are these wounds in thine hands? Then he shall answer, Those with which I was wounded in the house of my friends: (KJV). The question here is, "How many people in the history of the world have died with wounds in their hands?" I believe we can safely assume the chance of any person dying with wounds in his or her hands is somewhat greater than 1 in 1,000.

The sixth prophecy in Isaiah 53: 7 states, "He was oppressed and treated harshly, yet he never said a word. He was led like a lamb to the slaughter. And as a sheep is silent before the shearers, he did not open his mouth" (NLT). This raises a particularly tough question. How many people in the history of the world can we imagine being put on trial, knowing they were innocent, without making one statement in their defense? For our statistical model, let's say this is 1 in 1,000, although it is pretty hard to imagine.

Moving on to the seventh prophecy, Isaiah 53: 9 says "He had done no wrong and had never deceived anyone. But he was buried like a criminal; he was put in a rich man's grave" (NLT). Here we need to consider how many people, out of all the good individuals in the world who have died, have died a criminal's death and been buried in a rich person's grave? These people died out of place. (Some might also infer that they were buried out of place, though that is not necessarily true.) Let's assume the chance of a good person dying as a criminal and being buried with the rich is about 1 in 1,000.

The eighth and final prophecy is from Psalm 22: 16: "My enemies surround me like a pack of dogs; an evil gang closes in on me. They have pierced my hands and feet" (NLT). Remember this passage and all the other prophetic references to the crucifixion were written before this form of execution was invented. However, for our purposes, we just need to consider the probability of someone in the history of the world being executed by crucifixion. Certainly, Jesus wasn't the only person killed by being crucified. We will say that the chances of a person dying from this specific form of execution to be at 1 in 10,000.

Calculating the Results

To determine the chance that all these things would happen to the same person by chance, we simply need to multiply the fraction of each of the eight probabilities. When we do, we get a chance of 1 in 10^{28}. In other words, the probability is 1 in 10,000,000,000,000,000,000,000,000,000. Would you bet against these odds?

Unfortunately, there is another blow coming for those who do not believe the Bible is true or Jesus is who He said He was. There are not just eight prophecies of this nature in the Bible that were fulfilled in Jesus Christ------there are *more than three hundred* such prophecies in the Old Testament. The prophecies we looked at were just the ones that we could *most easily* show fulfilled.

If we deal with only forty-eight prophecies about Jesus, based on the above numbers, the chance that Jesus is not who He said He was or the Bible is not true is 1 in 10^{168}. This is a larger number than most of us can grasp (though you may want to try to write it sometime). To give you some perspective on just how big this number is, consider these statistics from the book *Science Speaks* by Peter Stoner:

- If the state of Texas were buried in silver dollars two feet deep, it would be covered by 10^{17} silver dollars.

- In the history of the world, only 10^{11} people have supposedly ever lived. (I don't know who counted this.)

- There are 10^{17} seconds in 1 billion years.

- Scientists tell us that there are 10^{66} atoms in the universe and 10^{80} particles in the universe.

- Looking at just forty-eight prophecies out of more than three hundred, there is only a 1 in 10^{168} chance of Jesus not being who He said He was or of the Bible being wrong.

In probability theory, the threshold for an occurrence being absurd---translate that as "impossible"---is only 10^{50}. No thinking person who understands these probabilities can deny the reality of our faith or the Bible based on intellect. Every person who has set out to disprove the Judeo-Christian Scriptures on an empirical basis has ended up proving the Bible's authenticity and has, in most cases, become a believer.

These facts are more certain than any others in the world. However, not everyone who has come to realize the reliability and reality of these documents has become a believer. These intelligent people who understand the statistical impossibility that Jesus was not who He claimed to be and who yet do not make a decision for Christ are not insane; they generally just have other issues. They allow these issues to stop them from enjoying the many experiential benefits that God offers them through His Word and the dynamic relationship they could have with Him, not to mention longer-term benefits. These people, of course, deserve love and prayer, because this is not just a matter of the intellect. If it were, every intelligent inquirer would be a believer. Rather, it is very much a matter of the heart, the emotions, and the spirit.

The truth of this statement was brought home to me in one very poignant situation. In this case, someone very near and dear to me said, "But Dad, this could have been anybody." No, this could not have been just anybody. The chance these prophecies could have been fulfilled in one person is so remote as to be absurd. That is impossible. Only one person in human history fulfilled these prophecies and that person is Jesus Christ. To claim otherwise is not intelligent, it is not smart, it is not well-considered, and it is not honest. It may be emotionally satisfying, but in all other respects it is self-delusional.

Printed in the United States
By Bookmasters